The Story of Saint George

*The Life and Legend
of
England's Patron Saint*

by
Anthony Cooney

First published in 1999 by This England Books,
Alma House, 73 Rodney Road, Cheltenham,
Gloucestershire GL50 1HT. Tel: 01242-537900.
This edition reprinted in 2008

Printed in Great Britain by Polestar Wheatons Ltd., Exeter

ISBN 0 906324 23 8

Contents

For my wife
Rita

INTRODUCTION

What English heart has not lifted at the sight of that brave but simple banner, the blood red Cross of Christ upon the white field of Eternity? It has led the progresses of kings, princes and prelates. It has decked the festivities of yeomen and peasants. It flutters in the breeze of an English April morning and boldly snaps in a spring gale. It has flown from church tower and village hall across all the shires of England. It is the Cross of St. George, the Banner of England.

And not only English hearts have lifted at its sight, for the Royal Navy has carried this banner across the seven seas: a sign of hope to the oppressed and of liberation to the enslaved. It has stood on watch upon the narrow seas of the Straits of Dover and upon the storm-lashed waves of the Lizard, a stern warning and challenge to the tyrant that he can never achieve his evil ends until he has first overthrown it, for this is the flag which has never bowed, the flag of liberty, the proud banner of Justice and Freedom.

How sad it is then that so few Englishmen know who the true St. George was, and how he came to be England's Patron Saint. Yet this is nothing new. Over 100 years ago a little girl wrote:

> "Alas for St. George of England
> The valiant knight of old,
> Who slew the fiery dragon
> And of whom many tales are told.
> Although he is our Patron Saint
> We think nought of his day,
> And there is silence everywhere
> Where there ought to be grand display."

The little girl grew up to be Mrs. Clifford Mills, author of the famous patriotic story and play, *Where the Rainbow Ends.*

The play became an annual event, and I saw it as a child in 1943. Two years later I saw Laurence Olivier's splendid film of Shakespeare's *Henry V*, and these two experiences never quite left me. However, when I next saw the film with my wife in 1962, the realization came to us that few, if any people, even knew the date of St. George's Day.

From that realization, The St. George's Day Association was born. Using an old flat-bed duplicator we sent off a circular to some 50 magazines who we thought might be interested. One of these small magazines must have printed it, for out of the blue arrived a reporter from the *Daily Mail* to interview us. His report, which ran to five column inches, began:

> A 30-year-old British Railways clerk ... to make 40 million English folk take a pride in their patron saint. On 23rd April, St. George's Day, 30-year-old Mr. Anthony Cooney will turn up at his office wearing a red rose. And at a nearby school his wife Margaret will be taking classes with a red rose firmly pinned to her dress. The Cooneys, who have just formed the St. George's Day Association, want roses everywhere. In cars, on buses, on trains, in stores and outside buildings. They want St. George's Day to be a national holiday — and will try to get MPs to press for it ...

The *Daily Mail*'s coverage resulted in an invitation to appear on BBC's *The North at Six* for a very sympathetic interview. After all this publicity we were naïve enough to think that the battle was won and that from henceforth the roses and banners of St. George would be a common sight each April 23rd. Unhappily that was not the case. The English, or far too many of them, remain as mesmerized as ever by "Europeanism" and "Internationalism".

Each year since, the battle has had to be fought all over again. It has been an uphill struggle, and immense encouragement and satisfaction were given by *This England* when it awarded me The Silver Cross of St. George in its 21st Birthday issue of Spring, 1989. Two things have been gained. First, there is far more awareness of St. George's Day than there was back in 1962. Secondly, it has become clear that there are forces which are afraid of St. George's Day and a rebirth of English patriotism and this is reflected by the national media.

In the beginning my wife and I knew little of St. George. The real St. George, the legendary St. George and the fairy-tale St. George were very much mixed up for us, as they are for most people. Reading and research and writing over the past 35 years have enabled me to disentangle the confusion. This book is based upon articles I have written which have appeared in *This England*, *The Universe*, *Roman Chronicle*, *Chrysostom*, *Anglo-Orthodoxy*, *Home*, *The Ransomer*, *The Reminder*, *Christian Order*, *Faith*, *The Defender*, *Candour*, *New Britain*, *The Lantern*, *The Catholic Gazette*, *Heritage* (Australia) etc.

I am indebted to the Reverend H.S. Revill for his two articles in *The Standard of St. George* in 1966, which set me upon the trail of the real St. George, and to the little book by Fr. Mark Elvins, *St. George Who Was He?*, published in the 1980s which confirmed much of what I had written. I am also indebted for background information to Bede's *History of the English Church and People*, *Hadrian's Wall* by Breeze & Dobson, *Roman Britain* by I.A. Richmond, *The Beginnings of English Society* by Dorothy Whitelock, *The Emergence of England and Wales* by A.W. Wade-Evans, *Europe and the Faith* by Hilaire Belloc and *Rome, Britain and the Anglo-Saxons* by Nicholas Highham.

It is my hope that this little book will disentangle the story of St. George for others, that it will clarify the ramifications of that story and its full meaning for England, and that it will be a permanent reference book in the armoury of every patriot.

Anthony Cooney, Liverpool, 1999

CHAPTER ONE
A Birthday in Heaven

Thanks to the work of the distinguished scholar, K. Krumbacher*, it is now possible to sift the true facts of the life of St. George from the mass of legend which grew up around him. Krumbacher examined all the ancient Latin, Greek, Coptic and Syriac texts to establish where they agreed with each other and where they were confirmed by known historical events. The true story of St. George can be briefly told.

George was born at Lydda in the Vale of Sharon (Palestine) about 270 AD. His parents were Christians but his father had found favour with the Emperor. George joined the Roman Army and because of his father's friendship his career was set fair. He rose to the rank of Tribune of the Imperial Guard, a rank equivalent to that of our Colonel of the Regiment. The Emperor, Diocletian, incited by his heir-apparent, the Caesar Galerius, issued edicts against Christians.

Galerius has been described in ancient texts as "The wickedest man in the world", being given to drunkenness and debauchery. It is little wonder that he saw Christianity as a rebuke to his life-style and was determined to crush it. The first decree ordered the burning of the Scriptures and liturgical books and the closing of churches. The second decree required everyone in the Imperial Service or in public employment to render divine honours to the Emperor by sprinkling a pinch of incense on a lamp before his statue. All who refused were to be put to death.

George was in the Imperial capital of Nicomedia when this

---

* *Der heilige Georg* (January, 1911).

The Emperor Diocletian who was incited by his heir-apparent to issue edicts against Christians. This ultimately led to St. George being condemned to death.

decree was published. Boldly he tore it down and ripped it up. He was brought before the Emperor but instead of grovelling for pardon he pleaded for justice for his fellow Christians. Commanded to offer divine honours to the Emperor, he courageously refused, declaring *"I believe in Jesus Christ, who only is both God and Lord"*. St. Ambrose of Milan, whose account of St. George's martyrdom is one of the most trustworthy, tells us:

> George, the most faithful soldier of Jesus Christ, when religion was by others concealed, alone adventured to confess the Name of God, whose heavenly grace infused such constancy into him that he not only warned the tyrants, but was contemptuous of their tortures.

That George was tortured to persuade him to apostatize by sprinkling the incense, all the ancient texts agree. Steadfast in his Christian faith, George was finally judged obdurate and condemned to death. He was beheaded on 23rd April, 303 AD, and this date has ever since been kept as his Birthday in Heaven.

CHAPTER TWO
A Bogus Saint George

Edward Gibbon was one of those liberal intellectuals whose motto appears to be "My country, always wrong", and who are never so happy as when they are sneering at their country and "debunking" its beliefs and traditions. Gibbon himself was an intelligent and educated man whose English prose is brilliant and scintillating. Unfortunately this very brilliance persuades the stupid and shallow that if they parrot the sneering they will somehow become "intellectuals". There are plenty of such people around today, ever eager to cry "St. George never existed, your Patron Saint is a phoney".

Gibbon was the first to popularise the notion that St. George, the Patron Saint of England, was a myth, based historically upon an altogether different person — one "George of Cappadocia", a criminal who met his end at the hands of an outraged mob. The ultimate source of Gibbon's version is in one of the Greek texts which tells that George was born in Cappadocia in modern Turkey. His father having been martyred as a Christian, his mother fled with the infant George to her family in Lydda. This might be true and does not alter the facts of George's family and upbringing being in Lydda, though it does not accord with the general view, derived from the majority of the ancient texts, that George's father was in good standing with the Emperor and that he died in Lydda whilst George was quite young.

Who then was the other George, the "George of Cappadocia"? Fortunately we know as much about him as we do about the real Saint George. He was a man of humble origins, born over a fuller's shop in Cilicia. He grew up to be a type

The Emperor Constantine who, in 330 AD, dedicated a church to St. George in the city of Constantinople.

very familiar to us: the "wheeler-dealer" or "spiv". He grew rich by selling salt-pork in short measure to the Roman Army. When his dishonesty was discovered he fled to Cappadocia.

The Arian heresy was strongly established in Cappadocia and was favoured by the Imperial Court who saw it as a weapon against Orthodox Christianity. This other George judged it expedient to embrace it. He became very popular among the Arians and they chose him to be Archbishop of Alexandria. Established in Alexandria, the new archbishop set about giving himself monopolies in certain goods to the ruin of many of the city's merchants. He also persecuted Orthodox Christians and Pagans indiscriminately. Eventually the Imperial power intervened and imprisoned him, but the populace rose in fury, broke into the prison and murdered him, throwing his body into the sea.

The Arian faction inserted his name into the "Martyrology" of the Coptic Church and published a "Passion of St. George", confusing their late archbishop with the Martyr. In spite of the fact that Pope Gelasius condemned this account as being "written by heretics and schismatics", a Roman writer, Ammianus Marcellinus, perpetuated the confusion, and centuries later Gibbon gleefully fell upon his text. In our own time the story of the bogus St. George has been perpetuated by Robert Graves in his pseudo-history *Count Belisarius*.

St. George, as is now established, was martyred in 303 AD. The Emperor Constantine dedicated a church to him in his new city of Constantinople in 330 AD. A church in Syria dedicated to him dates from 346 AD, yet we know with equal certainty that the Arian George was murdered in 362 AD. In short, the real St. George lived and suffered death possibly before the imposter was even born, and certainly whilst he was still a child.

England then has no myth or imposter for its Patron Saint, but, as will be shown, one of the most illustrious of the martyrs, venerated from the time of his witness unto death in all the ancient patriarchates of the Church: Latin, Greek, Alexandrian and Antiochian.

CHAPTER THREE
The World of Saint George

I f you visit York Minster and descend into the foundations, you will find yourself in the remains of the
Roman basilica over which the cathedral was built. Here
in 306 AD Constantine the Great was acclaimed Emperor
of the Roman World by the Legions of Britain. Here he
received the news that in Rome Maxentius had seized the
Imperial throne and was preparing an army for the seizure
of Gaul. Here he planned the incredible march from York,
through Gaul and across the Mont Cenis pass, to the gates
of Rome.

His army drawn up before the walls of Rome, Constantine
was beset by doubt. His troops were weary. They had
marched across Europe; their weapons were worn from
fighting pitched battles at Turin and Verona, and in the
morning they must fight the decisive battle. That night Constantine remained awake in his tent, reading Virgil's *Eclogues*
where the poet laments the sorrows of the world — *"Sunt
lachrymae rerum"* — "The tears of things", but suddenly finds
cause for hope — a Saviour will be born, "The son of High
Jove", who will renew the world, and, says Virgil, the event
is so soon at hand that he himself hopes to live to see it.

Having read these verses, Constantine, upon an impulse,
stepped out of his tent and, looking up, saw a blazing cross in
the sky. Amazed, he heard the words: "By this sign shalt thou
conquer". At dawn he ordered his soldiers to paint the cross
upon their shields and prepare for battle. Maxentius emerged
from the city and deployed his army across the Milvian
Bridge. By evening, Maxentius had drowned in the Tiber,
Constantine had entered Rome as undisputed Emperor, and

The magnificent York Minster which dominates the city's sky-line. It was here, in 306 AD, that the Legions of Britain acclaimed Constantine, Emperor of the Roman World.

18

the history of the world was changed.

How did it come about that the greatest of the Roman Emperors was proclaimed in York, a city on the very fringe of the Empire, and what has he to do with St. George? Diocletian was made Emperor of Rome in 284 AD after almost a century of anarchy, mutiny and rebellion. The currency was debased, inflation rampant and trade stagnated. The cities had degenerated into crime-infested slums where the principle activities of idle mobs were protests, demonstrations and the daubing of graffiti on the decaying walls of the public buildings.

Diocletian was not primarily a soldier but he was a first-class administrator. He realized that he could not effectively govern the Empire from Rome; previous Emperors had indeed taken up residence in Milan to be nearer the Rhine frontier. The great centres of population, trade and manufacture were all in the Eastern Mediterranean: in Alexandria, Antioch and the cities of Greece and Asia Minor. In the West there were only two comparable seaports: Rome itself and Massala (the present-day Marseilles).

Diocletian's first step was to move his capital to Nicomedia in modern Turkey where he could guard against both the Persian Empire and the Barbarians from beyond the Danube. Next he divided the Empire into East and West, appointing a junior emperor, Maximian, to rule in the latter. Each "Empire" was further divided into two "Prefectures", one governed by the Emperor directly and the other by his adopted heir, who had the title of "Caesar". The idea of the Emperor adopting a man of proven abilities as his heir, to the exclusion of his own sons, had been successful in the 2nd century. Diocletian was well aware that the sons of emperors generally succumbed to the opportunities for luxury, idleness, evil company and vice which their position offered them and he believed that succession by adoption would again solve the problem of weak and unsuitable men becoming Emperor. The successor adopted by Diocletian was Galerius Valerius Maximus. The successor adopted by Maximian was Constantius Chlorus, nephew of Claudius II Gothicus. His Prefecture included Britain, France and Spain.

The army was also reorganized, being increased from about 300,000 men to over half-a-million. This made possible the creation, for the first time, of a mobile reserve of heavy cavalry ("knights") stationed behind the frontier forces. Two new kinds of administrator were introduced: "Dux" who were civil administrators, and "Comes" who were military leaders. When central authority collapsed in the West it was these Dukes and Counts who maintained order and civilization in their territories.

To consolidate his power and discourage rebellion, Diocletian adopted the Persian notion of the "Divine Emperor" who must not only be obeyed but worshipped by his subjects. This led him, in 303 AD, to unleash the last great persecution of Christianity. This then was the world in which St. George was martyred. We must now return to Britain and go back a little in time to understand how Constantine came to be in York.

In 287 AD one of Diocletian's new "Comes", Carausius, Count of the Saxon Shore and Admiral of Britain, decided that if there could be two Emperors there was no reason why there should not be three. He proclaimed himself Emperor and seized not only Great Britain, but also the Low Countries. He had no desire, however, as Constantine was to have, to march to Rome and make himself sole Emperor. His ambition was to create a Northern Empire with London as its capital. It is from Carausius, perhaps, that the idea of a sovereign Britain derives: an achievement attempted by two other Counts of Britain — Magnus Maximus (383 AD) and his son, Constantine III (407 AD). Though they failed, the idea was never abandoned and was succinctly put 1,000 years later in Thomas Cromwell's dictum "Britain is an Empire" — that is, not a tributary kingship in a larger Imperium, but an Empire itself.

Diocletian and Maximian, having no resources immediately

Cardiff City Hall. The Welsh capital was founded by Carausius to guard the west coast of Britain.

available to put down the rebellion, were forced to recognize Carausius as a brother emperor. Carausius marked this recognition by issuing fine silver *denarii* stamped with the heads of the three Emperors in silhouette. Roman Emperors frequently used their coinage as propaganda, as we shall see.

Carausius was an able administrator. He built a chain of forts and fortified towns along the Saxon Shore, and to guard the west coast founded Cardiff and Lancaster. These forts had mixed garrisons of soldiers and sailors for intercepting raiders both on land and sea and were bases for sea-patrols. His new fine silver coinage restored confidence in trade and London became a busy port. This made a re-conquest of Britain a formidable task and Rome was forced to bide its time.

In 293 AD Carausius was assassinated by Alectus, his chief finance officer, who proclaimed himself Emperor. Anarchy followed and Rome seized its opportunity. In 296 AD Constantius Chlorus Caesar successfully landed his legions in Britain and defeated Alectus. The victor established his headquarters at York where his son, Constantine, joined him. In 305 AD Constantius succeeded Maximian as Emperor, but was unable to leave for Rome before his death in 306 AD. On the death of his father, Constantine was proclaimed Emperor in the basilica of York.

We may now consider the second question. What had Constantine to do with St. George?

There are several connections between Constantine and St. George, though the verified ones are after the martyrdom of the latter. Nevertheless, the known facts of Constantine's career lend credence to some of the British legends which have grown up about both men. Legends are not to be taken at face value, but neither are they to be dismissed out of hand for they usually have a basis of fact. Let us consider the known facts of Constantine's life.

Constantine was born about 274 AD, the exact year is uncertain, in Naissus, Upper Moesia. He was the son of Constantius Chlorus and Helena, known to us as St. Helen. He first distinguished himself as a soldier in Diocletian's Egyptian expedition of 296 AD. He next served with Galerius Caesar in the Persian war. When Diocletian and Maximian abdicated to make way for their chosen heirs, Constantine left the East and joined his father, now "Augustus of the West", in an expedition against the Picts. Constantius Chlorus, knowing that he was dying, gave his son the title of "Caesar" and declared him his successor. Galerius, though acknowledging Constantine's title, refused to recognize him as co-Emperor. This encouraged Maxentius, son of the retired Maximian, to proclaim himself Emperor in the West. This brought his father, who does not appear to have had any great faith in his son's abilities or character, out of retirement to reassume the purple. There were now three "Emperors" in the West!

This grab-what-you-can-whilst-the-going-is-good mentality

seems to have been catching, for two men also challenged Galerius in the East: Licinius and another Maximian. The Empire now had six Emperors! All the care of Diocletian to ensure a capable and worthy succession lay in the ruins of ambition and greed. Maxentius drove his father out of Rome and the latter  committed suicide. As we have seen, Maxentius next prepared to seize Gaul but was eventually defeated at the Milvian Bridge. This left Constantine undisputed Emperor of the West. Meanwhile in the East, Galerius had the unusual distinction of dying a natural death in 311 AD and in 313 AD Licinius defeated Maximian who died in prison, leaving Licinius undisputed Emperor of the East.

The Edict of Milan (313 AD), issued jointly by Constantine and Licinius, ended the persecution of Christianity. This promising start of co-operation did not last, however. War broke out between the co-Emperors in 314 AD and Licinius was forced to cede Illyricum, Pannonia and Greece to the West. In 323 AD Constantine again defeated Licinius and put him to death. He was now sole Emperor of the Roman World. In 324 AD he made Christianity the official religion of the Empire and called the first General Council of the Church, at Nicaea (325 AD). He commenced building a new capital, Constantinople, the first entirely Christian city, which was completed in 330 AD. Shortly before his death in 337 AD he himself embraced Christianity and was baptized.

The British legends surrounding Constantine are interesting because they show the beginnings of a sense of national identity and national pride. The legends claim that St. Helen was a British Princess. "Reputable" history says that Helena was born in Bithynia, the daughter of an innkeeper, and that

Constantius divorced her in 292 AD in order to marry the daughter of Maximian. The British legend has it that she was the daughter of King Coel, born in Colchester.

On the side of the British legend it must be said that our knowledge of Helena's origins is not cut and dried and is open to dispute. It can be argued that a British princess is a more likely bride for the nephew of an Emperor and rising star of the Empire than would be the daughter of an innkeeper. Helena's energy and intelligence as Empress-Dowager certainly show her to have been a remarkable woman, one used to exercising authority and leadership. On the other hand it is argued that the British legend confuses Helena with another Helen, the wife of Magnus Maximus.

The British legend continues to say that Constantius, serving in Britain, had married Helena but had been recalled to Rome whilst she was expecting her first-born. According to this legend, therefore, Constantine — the greatest of the Roman Emperors — was born in Britain of a British mother. Further, King Coel prophesied that this British child would rule over all the land he rode upon. The revolt of Carausius, among other things, prevented Constantius returning to Britain. In Rome he was forced to divorce Helena and marry Maximian's daughter.

Constantine, meanwhile, remained in Britain with his mother at the Court of King Coel, and so was brought up and educated as a British prince. Certainly, Constantine's first act upon becoming Emperor was to bestow upon his mother the Imperial names and titles — "Helena Julia Flavia Augusta, Dowager Empress of Rome", which argues a closeness between mother and son and the son's determination to recompense her for his father's desertion.

As we have seen, the young Constantine followed his father into the army, being posted to the Court of Diocletian. Upon the retirement of Diocletian, Galerius became Emperor of the East. Constantine, so the legend runs, realizing his danger as one of those whom the wicked Galerius needed to eliminate, made good his escape and rode across Europe to York. So, continues the legend, Constantine rode from Nicomedia on the eastern fringes of the Empire to York on its western fringes, and over all this territory, as King Coel had prophesied, he, a British Prince, came to rule.

If Coel's prophecy is legend, Constantine's journey is fact. Another British legend has it that Constantine and St. George were friends and companions-in-arms. Here again the known facts and the legend coincide. Constantine *was* in the service of Diocletian in 296 AD at the time that George was Tribune of the Imperial Guard, and they could hardly have failed to meet. We will look more closely at this legend when we come to consider the English legend of St. George.

CHAPTER FOUR
The Fame of Saint George

"Gleams the strong palace of the noble martyr George,
Whose honour strews the whole wide world,
Confessing Christ through bars, bloodshed and thirst,
By bonds, by hunger, cold and searing flames,
His head he raised to dwell 'mid glittering stars.
In valour mighty, tombed beneath eastern heavens,
Lo, 'neath western skies he offers help.
Therefore, remember, you who pass by,
To lift your hearts in prayer, and pay your vows
For here, by its well deserving, honest faith
Wins that which with eagerness it seeks.
Let the souls who His new temples are,
Forward advance along His saint's straight way."

So wrote Venantius Fortunatus, Bishop of Poitiers in the mid 6th century, better known today for his hymn *Vexilla Regis*. His poem is testimony to the widespread fame of St. George within a century of his martyrdom.

After his execution, the friends of St. George recovered his body and took it to his beloved Lydda where they buried it and planted a rose-bush on the grave. That, one might think, would be the end of the story; George, after all, was one martyr among an estimated two million in the first three centuries of Christianity. Edward Gibbon, in his sneering way, has referred to this holocaust as "the annual consumption of martyrs" and maintained that the number was greatly exaggerated. However there can be little doubt that the number of martyrs was considerable and to those who died must be added all those who

The village of Lydda, birthplace of St. George.

were imprisoned, tortured and driven into exile.

St. George's burial, however, was not the end of his story but rather the beginning. After Constantine had gained control of the Eastern Empire he built a church on the site of St. George's martyrdom, the ruins of which are still known to the local population as "The mosque of St. George". He built a second church over the saint's grave at Lydda.

Lydda, 23 miles from Jerusalem, became a bishopric. The town grew famous as a place of pilgrimage to the tomb of "The Great Martyr". A Church Council was held there in 415 AD for the purpose of trying the British monk Pelagius for heresy. Briefly, Pelagius taught that salvation could be earned by good works alone, and not by the Grace of God. As Bede tells us, it was a particularly widespread heresy in Roman Britain, calling for a visit by St. Germanus of the Gallic Church to suppress it. It would be extraordinary if British bishops and divines did not attend this Council, and we may make an intelligent guess that if the cult of St. George had not already reached Britain by that time, it would be brought here by those returning from the Council.

The earliest reference to St. George is that of Eusebius, Patriarch of Constantinople. Eusebius had been a contemporary of St. George, and Nicomedia was in his diocese. In 338 AD, just 35 years after George's death, he wrote:

> Immediately on the promulgation of the edict a certain man of no mean origin, but highly esteemed for his temporal dignities, as soon as the decree was published against the churches in Nicomedia, stimulated by a divine zeal and excited by ardent faith, took it as it was openly placed and posted up for public inspection, and tore it to shreds as a most profane and wicked act. This, too, was done when the two Caesars were in the city, the first of whom was the eldest and chief of all, and the other held fourth grade of the imperial dignity after him. But this man, as the first that was distinguished there in this manner, after enduring what was likely to follow an act so daring, preserved his mind, calm and serene until the moment when his spirit fled.
>
> (Trans. S. Baring-Gould, *Lives of the Saints*, 1897)

Historians are satisfied that Eusebius is talking about St. George. It has been objected that he does not mention the name of the "Man of no mean origin". It is equally true that he does not mention the names of the "Two Caesars" — Diocletian and Galerius. To my mind this absence of names argues the validity of the account. Let anyone recall some event which happened in their lifetime and consider how different is their knowledge of that event compared with their knowledge of things which happened before they were born. Part of the difference is the feeling that what they know about something they lived through is known to everyone else; they can talk about it without unnecessary explanation and detail. Eusebius feels no need for names — everyone in Constantinople knew that Diocletian was the Emperor and Galerius the Caesar. Everyone knew that George was among the first of the martyrs. Another contemporary account already mentioned is that of St. Ambrose, Bishop of Milan.

As the fame of George spread, so too a number of "Lives" of the saint began to be circulated in the Latin, Greek, Coptic, Syrian, Armenian and Ethiopian churches. The first of these purported to be written by one Pasicrates, the servant of St.

St. George has been immortalized in many different ways. This cigarette card shows an 18th-century Staffordshire pottery figure.

S. GEORGE & THE DRAGON.

George. The claim by an author to have been the servant of his hero was a frequently used literary device of the time. This may seem dishonest to us but to authors of an earlier age it was an entirely acceptable way of saying "If this book had been written by one who knew its hero, this is exactly what he would have written"!

Needless to say, historians, Krumbacher among them, do not give any credence to the unknown author's claim to be Pasicrates and St. George's servant. This does not mean that the text does not contain much useful information and it also serves to establish when and where wild exaggeration and alteration began to creep into later texts. The *Enconium* of Theodotus, Bishop of Ancyra, relies upon Pasicrates for details of St. George's imprisonment, torture and death, but gives us other interesting information. For example, we are told that his mother was the daughter of the Count of Lydda and a descendant of "The saints at Lydda and Sharon" whom St. Peter visited (Acts ix: 32-35). The *Enconium* also tells us that George, having joined the army, served with Galerius in the Persian campaign for two years, in which, as we have seen, Constantine also served. We also find that George was offered bland-

29

St. George's church in the Surrey village of Crowhurst. One of the windows also features England's patron saint on horseback.

ishments of wealth and rank if he would but acknowledge the divinity of the Emperor by sprinkling incense before his statue.

The *Enconium* was followed by other texts, dependent upon Pasicrates but given to exaggeration and fantasy. According to some of these later texts St. George was tortured for a period of seven years, however to no avail, for not only would George not sacrifice to the Genius of the Emperor, but after these tortures he was miraculously made whole. Meanwhile George was playing no passive part. In the midst of the most horrible tortures he worked some astounding miracles, including raising several people from the dead. Finally he caused all the pagan idols to crash in ruins before him and this converted Diocletian's wife, the Empress Alexandra, to Christianity. This so enraged Diocletian that he ordered her to be put to death and St. George to be beheaded.

In the Latin version, Galerius becomes the "Emperor Dacian

30

of Persia", whilst a later version describes "Dacian" as "Pro-Consul". This is interesting because Galerius Caesar was in fact a Dacian, a territory which became the modern Romania, and his rank as Caesar could be described as "Pro-Consul" by someone not familiar with the history of the 3rd-century Empire. In short, these slips point to an author relying upon sources he only half understands and consequently distorts.

By the end of the 5th century, churchmen were becoming concerned about these exaggerations, and in 494 AD Pope Gelasius, as already mentioned, issued a decree rejecting all of these fabulous stories and warning that George was "to be numbered among those saints whose names are justly reverenced among men, but whose actions are known only to God". This decree is in itself sufficient to dispose of the confusion with the bogus "saint", George of Cappadocia, for Gelasius would hardly have described an Arian heretic as one whose name is "justly reverenced among men".

These apocryphal "Lives" of St. George, however embroidered, however exaggerated they may be, tell us something of importance. They tell us that the fame of St. George as a martyr in the last great persecution of Christianity had spread far and wide, and had done so in a remarkably short space of time.

The question arises as to *why* the fame and the cult of St. George spread so far and so rapidly and why so many churches in all parts of the Christian world were dedicated to him so soon? The answer may be found perhaps in the words of St. Ambrose and in the efforts of his persecutors to persuade him to worship the Emperor. Let us look again at what St. Ambrose had to say:

> George, the most faithful soldier of Jesus Christ, when religion was by others concealed, alone adventured to confess the Name of God...

In other words, after 300 years something of the zeal of the first Christians had been lost. The Christians of the 3rd century had been *born* Christians, but they had careers, homes, property, wealth, just like any of their pagan neighbours. Is a pinch of incense really such a big deal compared with losing all of these? After all, one doesn't need to *mean* anything by sprinkling the incense before the Emperor's statue: one can always say "baloney" under one's breath! So "religion was concealed" in the hope that the heart could still feel the same after formal apostasy as it had before.

What a prize, George, Tribune of the Imperial Guard, man of noble family and substantial wealth would be for the enemies of Christianity! Where he led, others would surely flock. On the other hand, how fatal to the success of the campaign against Christianity would be his continued defiance. We may say that George lost his head when all about him were saving theirs, and in return received a crown.

Here, I am convinced, is the reason for St. George's fame and for its rapid spread. George *"alone confessed the Name of God, whose heavenly grace infused such constancy into him, that he not only warned the tyrants, but was contemptuous of their tortures"*. George yielded neither to bribes nor torture, and his example saved the Church. Those who were wavering became resolute and the persecution failed. Within a few years of George's martyrdom, Galerius and Diocletian were dead, Constantine was Emperor, the indefatigable St. Helen was building the churches on the Mount of Olives and in Bethlehem (and finding, many believe, the true cross), Christianity was the official religion of the Empire and persecution ceased.

It is for this reason that the Greek Church honours St. George under the title of "Captain of the Noble Army of Martyrs". The Coptic Church hails him as "The Trophy Bearer". In the West he is named as "Champion of Christendom". In his native Palestine he is Patron of Healing, especially of lunacy, and is honoured as such even by Muslims. Because his name means "husbandman" ("Geo" — Earth; "Ergos" — Worker) he is the Patron Saint of Agriculture. He was a soldier and so is the Patron Saint of Soldiers, particularly of cavalry.

He laid down his life in the very springtime of manhood and so is the exemplar of all that is courageous and noble, the protector of youth and of chastity. Because he acted courageously to succour the oppressed and plead their cause he is hailed as "Aid of the helpless". He is regarded as protector of those in peril from storm and tempest at sea, and merchants invoked his protection and chose him as their saint; in Italy the first bank was formed by the merchants of Genoa who named it "The Bank of St. George". Beside being Patron Saint of England, St. George is also Patron Saint of Catalonia and Georgia, and it is significant that both are marcher kingdoms of Christendom, watch-towers upon her borders. This, then, is the fame of St. George whom we are proud to hail as our Patron and Protector and about whom we have created a special and entirely English legend to make him our own.

CHAPTER FIVE
The English Saint George

I n *Royal Windsor* (1879), Hepworth Dixon says:

> *England has established St. George throughout the earth; on every ocean we have borne his flag, on every island we have reared his fame. We gave his name to St. George's Channel, the stormy inlet of the Irish Sea. The direct peril on the Atlantic Ocean we have called "St. George's Bank". From Behring Straits to Maine, from Florida to Patagonia, we have set him up on guard. Penang, Tasmania, Western Australia keep up the memory of the soldier-martyr, St. George, the Patron Saint of England.*

I have suggested already that St. George's connection with England begins before the Anglo-Saxon settlement and long, long before the Norman Conquest or the Crusades, with his friendship with Constantine the Great. It is true that there is no direct documentary evidence of a friendship between the future martyr and the future Emperor, but it is certain that both George and Constantine served under Diocletian in Egypt at approximately the same time, and under Galerius for two years in the Persian war. As both were high-ranking officers it would be astonishing indeed if they did not meet and did not work together. It is upon this deduction that the legend of St. George serving in Britain is based.

The difference between tradition and legend on the one hand and fairy tale on the other, is that the former is usually found to rest upon and enshrine facts. There may be a mix-up of persons with similar names or events of a similar nature, but study and research are able to tease out the truth. What is amazing is the length of time a legend can be handed down from generation to generation, more or less intact.

The outstanding example of this is, of course, the Siege of Troy. The story must have been passed on by word of mouth for hundreds of years before Homer set it in verse, and then his great epic was transmitted from memory for hundreds of years before it was eventually written down. Because the *Iliad* mentioned things, such as bronze weapons, war-chariots and body-length shields, unknown in Classical Greece, the "intellectuals" dismissed it as fiction, until that is Schliemann went to Turkey, started digging, and found Troy. Today, even the wine-shop by the gates, where Homer says the warriors paused for a draught of wine, has been identified.

Another example is the legend of the "labyrinth", and the youths and maidens sacrificed to the man-bull monster, the minotaur. This also was regarded as fantasy, until Sir Arthur Evans excavated Knossos to reveal the maze of cellars and corridors, the murals of the bull-dancers, the great "figure of eight" shields, and the bull-mask with crystal eyes worn by Minos on ceremonial occasions.

One last example of the persistence of memory over millennia, let alone centuries, is that of Pylos. When archaeologists, early in this century, arrived on the island to search for the palace of Nestor, the local people shrugged their shoulders, pointed to a mound and said: "There it is". And there it was! The fairy story, on the other hand, although it conveys moral and psychological truths, does so by fantasy. There are both legends and fairy stories concerning St. George's connection with England.

According to tradition, St. George was posted to York, the headquarters of Constantius Chlorus Caesar. The tradition is specific: George landed at Porta Sisuntorium, the modern Lancaster, the nearest port on the west coast to York. This is an important detail which supports the legend, for as we have seen, Porta Sisuntorium was founded by Carausius and it was only after the restoration of Imperial rule that Constantius established himself at York, which makes the date of George's arrival accurate.

Glastonbury Tor in Somerset. According to legend, St. George travelled to this spot after he was posted to York.

At York, George and Constantine renewed their friendship, and, the legend has it, visited Glastonbury and the tomb of Joseph of Arimathea. Finally George received a second posting to Caerleon-on-Usk, the headquarters of the II Augusta, before being recalled to Nicomedia in time to tear down the edicts against the Christians.

There is nothing improbable about this tradition, indeed it has a great deal of support. Even if there was no friendship between Constantine and George, a posting to the court of Constantius Chlorus would be eagerly sought by an ambitious young officer aspiring to higher rank. Add to that the high probability that Constantine and George were friends, and we have an even more pressing motive to seek such a posting. If we grant that George was at York, a pilgrimage to Glastonbury would be certain, especially if George believed Joseph of Arimathea to be among his forefathers ("The saints at Lydda and Sharon"). There is also a strong local tradition along the South Wales border of George's service with the II Augusta. We must finally remember Constantine's building of two churches, over the site of George's martyrdom and over his grave. Such remembrance would hardly be lavished on a stranger and argues for a true and upright, lifelong friendship, between these noble Romans.

The next stage in the development of the legend links the cult of St. George with the legendary King Arthur and the Knights of the Round Table. This, I must admit, was new to me until I came across it in articles by S.M.M. Crichton in *Verity* (Spring 1964) and the Reverend H.S. Revill in *The Standard of St. George* (April 1966). Let them speak for themselves. Crichton writes:

> All this however is very far away and does not explain why a saint, who seems to have lived entirely in the East, comes to be our Patron Saint. King Arthur appears to have been the first to bring his name to England. About two-hundred years after the death of the saint, King Arthur formed his company of the Knights of the Round Table, with St. George as their ideal and pattern. In all the strange half-legendary, half-true stories of King Arthur and his Knights, it is easy to see how St. George came to be their natural hero.

37

Revill writes:

Perhaps the earliest form of the Order (i.e. the Order of the Garter) of which we know can be traced to the institution of "The Order of the Society of St. George and the Round Table" founded by King Arthur. It was approximately two-hundred years after the martyrdom of St. George that Arthur set about founding his Order of Chivalry with St. George as its Patron.

I have been unable to find sources, such as an historian would require, for these assertions, and I am inclined to think that they are based upon an embroidering, after the event, of the original, sounder tradition of St. George's friendship with Constantine and service in Britain. Even so, this legend would still be evidence of the pride and affection in which Englishmen held St. George. I also think that as legends usually have a basis of truth we should give them all the weight they can bear.

Readers will recall that it was suggested that the cult of St. George may have been brought to Britain as early as 415 AD by bishops and divines returning from the Council of Lydda. Now let us look at King Arthur and his Knights of the Round Table. Arthur has been identified by Professor John Rhys as one of the two Roman Britons appointed by Aetius, Prefect of Gaul, to organize the defence of Britain against marauding Picts and Scots after the withdrawal of the legions. Professor Rhys suggests that Arthur falls readily into the place and position of "Count of Britain", and the Welsh historian, A.W. Wade Evans, has suggested that the other would be Octa, "Count of the Saxon Shore". In the early texts Arthur is never styled "Gwledig", that is "Rex" in the Roman sense, but is described as having fought "along with the kings (*reges*) of the Britons". That Arthur organized the defence exceptionally well is witnessed by Gildas in his *De Excidio*.

And then it was that they began to inflict on their foes, who for many years had been plundering the land, great slaughter. They trusted not in men, but in God.

The Knights of the Round Table also fall readily into place as a mobile brigade of heavy cavalry, such as those introduced

St. George's church in the Yorkshire town of Doncaster. A church dedicated to the nation's patron saint has stood in this town since the 7th century.

by Diocletian's army reforms, composed of Roman Britons of equestrian rank. However Gildas's words imply a religious dimension — "they trusted not in men but in God" — which supports the assertion that they were a dedicated order under the Patronage of St. George, exemplar of Christian virtue, chivalry and manhood.

The dedication of a church in Doncaster to St. George in the early 7th century confirms that his cult was known in Britain, as does the fact that his name was included in the canon of the Anglo-Saxon Mass. St. Bede (673-735) entered his feast for 23rd April in the "Martyrology" he compiled.

From this point on, however, we move into an area of legend (of which the Arthurian references may be the beginning) which gradually becomes fairy tale. Both the later legends and the fairy tales are clearly intended to Anglicise St. George, to make him "One of us". In the year 1,000 AD St. Aelfric published a "life" which has George "a rich ealdorman", from the "Shire of Cappadocia". Later still George's birthplace becomes "Coventry" and his father is "Lord Albert".

39

In many parts of England, mumming plays are still performed and the story of St. George and the dragon proves to be a perennial favourite. Here, one of the Furness Morris Men takes on the Saint's role and issues his challenge to the Prince of Paradise.

At this point, St. George becomes a fairy-tale figure rather than a Christian saint. As his story unfolds it transpires that he is a Saxon prince, stolen by the fairies and abandoned in a furrow. Here he is found by a farmer, who with his wife adopts him as his own, naming him "George" after the earth in which he was discovered. When he is grown up his true identity is discovered, for blood will out, and he becomes the "Red Cross Knight" of Spenser's *Faerie Queen*, a champion of King Arthur.

The dragon as a fire-breathing monster now appears in the story. St. George, the English knight-errant on a pilgrimage to Jerusalem, encounters the dragon in either Egypt or Libya, where it is about to devour the Princess Sabra (also known as "Cliodolinda" and "Elya"). George slays the dragon, rescues the princess, marries her and returns to Coventry. Here George and his wife have three sons, the most famous being Sir Guy of Warwick, who also slays dragons.

How deeply the legend of St. George as an English knight-errant had entered the national consciousness is eloquently testified to by the repeated invocations of his name in Shakespeare's *Henry V*, but there is still later evidence of this strong and persistent folk conviction.

In the 17th century a new chapter was added to the popular story. Princess Sabra having been killed in a riding accident, a grieving St. George makes a second pilgrimage to Jerusalem. Returning, he finds another dragon wasting England. He gives battle and slays the monster, but overcome by the poison it spews upon him, he also dies. This final encounter takes place either on Dunsmore Heath (Warwickshire), at Uffington (Berkshire), Brinsop (Herefordshire) or the hamlet of St. George (Denbighshire) — all are eager to lay claim to the honour. It is this second dragon-slaying in England which is represented in the mumming plays, still popular in the 19th century and recorded by Thomas Hardy in *The Return of the Native*.

The dragons introduced into the story in the 11th century may be reminiscent of the Viking dragon ships and their

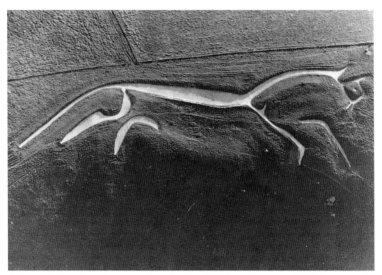

The distinctive landmark of the White Horse of Uffington in Berkshire. Later versions of the legend of St. George point to this as being one of the possible locations for the brave knight's last encounter with a dragon.

plundering raids, but truly in the development of the story after the Norman Conquest we can see an assertion of the national spirit. St. George has become the symbol of English resistance to continental occupation. He is the rallying point for Englishmen, his story one which stirs the heart with pride against the arrogance of the contemptuous Normans and their 11th-century "EU".

If the real St. George has been obscured by this fairy-tale figure, the fairy tale is nevertheless testimony to the affection in which the English held St. George until recent times. One of Rossetti's most splendid paintings is *The Wedding of St. George and Princess Sabra* (1857), now in the Tate Gallery, London. St. George is presented pre-eminently as an Englishman, the St. George of Spenser's fairy epic, of the mumming plays and of Mrs. Clifford Mills's *Where the Rainbow Ends* — "Golden-haired, blue-eyed, English of the English". It was doubtless this St. George who the commanding officer of the Royal Marines had in mind when he led the Zeebrugge raid on St. George's Day, 1918. Leaping onto the bullet-spattered quay he encouraged his men with the cry: *"Saint George for England, let's twist the dragons' tails"*. In the event the "dragons" (German submarines) were successfully destroyed in their lairs.

The courage of the Royal Marines on that St. George's Day gives the lie to the defeatist story, pedalled by the chattering classes in recent years, that by 1918 disillusion and despair had replaced patriotism and courage among Englishmen.

In our own time it was on St. George's Day, 1982, that the Royal Marines stormed ashore on South Georgia and Admiral Woodward sent his eagerly-awaited signal:

Make to the Lords of the Admiralty. Be pleased to inform Her Majesty that the White Ensign flies alongside the Union Jack on South Georgia. God Save the Queen.

"Superior" persons may dismiss St. George of England as a "myth", but the cosmopolitan, rootless "intellectuals" miss the real point which generations of their unlettered kin know by the instinct of the heart whenever they hoist the Red Cross Banner of England. The legend is the *truth*: St. George, dauntless, courteous, knightly, is the type and figure of all our race and kind. He is what Englishmen aspire to be.

CHAPTER SIX
Where the Rainbow Ends

The remarkable and beautiful fairy story, *Where the Rainbow Ends* by Mrs. Clifford Mills, sounded a warning note at the very beginning of the 20th century which has, unhappily, been more than justified.

The story concerns two children, Crispian, a Royal Naval cadet, and his sister Rosamund. Very much a hero in his own right is their pet English lion cub, "Cubby". Their parents have been lost at sea, returning from India, and their guardian, Cousin Matthew, has died suddenly, so they come under the care of the wicked Uncle Joseph and his sister, Aunt Matilda. Uncle Joseph is determined to sell the children's home, pocket the money, and take Cris out of the Royal Navy to employ him as an office boy in his own firm. It is at this point that Rosamund remembers "The Rainbow Book" which tells of the "Land Where All Lost Loved Ones Are Found". The book relates that they must travel through the kingdom of the Dragon King, and to reach the frontiers of this dread region they must find Faith's Magic Carpet.

She convinces Cris that the carpet in Cousin Matthew's library is indeed the magic carpet, and they summon the genie who tells them that they must each make two wishes. Cris wishes for his friend from Dartmouth, the Scot, Blunders, and his sister, Betty. Rosamund, hearing Uncle Joseph and Aunt Matilda coming in from dinner, wishes that they have dinner served all over again. Then, with a sudden inspiration she wishes for St. George of England. A hermit appears in the room. The children are terribly disappointed, but the hermit explains that he is indeed St. George, but he has been banished and neglected by Englishmen who have been blinded by the gold-dust the Dragon King has thrown in their eyes.

Rosamund and Betty beg his protection against the Dragon King, and immediately he is transformed into the knight they imagined him to be. Just as the wicked Uncle and Aunt are about to enter the library, the children with Cubby and St. George order the carpet away and, with a flash of light, it begins its journey. Unfortunately William, the boot-boy, and a sneak and coward, has been hiding behind the curtains all the time. He has heard the genie warn that if anyone tears away so much as a thread of Faith's carpet, he can summon the Dragon King to pursue them. William snatches a thread from the carpet as it rises and presents it to the evil Joseph. Uncle Joseph makes his first appearance in the book hiding Cubby's "Colonial Mixture", for he knows that this makes British Lions grow strong. Let the book tell Joseph's reasons in its own words.

> If Cubby had been an American lion or an Asiatic lion or a German or a French lion, Uncle Joseph wouldn't have minded a bit how enormous he had grown, but he just hated anything belonging to his own nation to be big or strong or powerful — and yet, if ever lions of other countries wanted to hurt him or take anything of his, he expected the British Lion he did his best to starve, to protect him and fight the other lions for him.

Uncle Joseph lives up to this introduction to his character. He summons the Dragon King without hesitation. The Dragon King is delighted to obey, as he later explains to Dunks, his Prime Minister:

> "These children have, to shield them from my wrath, invoked the aid of their own Patron Saint, my mortal enemy, St. George. He whose spirit it has been my plan to deaden in the hearts of Englishmen. Almost had I worked the downfall of his land — I flung my gold-dust in the people's eyes and lulled them into false security. Yes, I had won — but honour, so slight a thing I deemed her nought, did from this death sleep bid the land arise, and at her call Britain's Empire woke, and hailing my enemy as her champion led him out once more on life's arena. To what heights has he not led Britons in the past, to what greater heights may he not lead them in the future!"

45

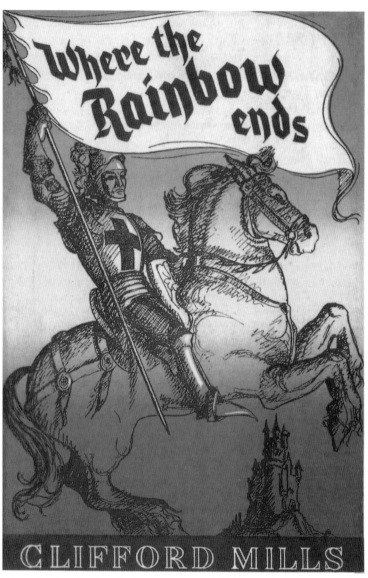

The children's book "Where the Rainbow Ends" was first published in 1911 and provided many youngsters with an introduction to St. George. The story was last reprinted more than 30 years ago.

46

However, by the time the Dragon King with Uncle Joseph and Aunt Matilda catch up with the children they are safely on St. George's ground on the very edge of the Dragon Wood. Here where the Red Cross of England floats on the breeze the Dragon King is powerless, so he storms off into the woods to plan how he can lure the children into his domain during the hours of darkness. Uncle Joseph, however, thinks patriotism and flags a lot of rubbish and is not the least bit afraid to rush onto St. George's ground and seize the children:

"Oh dearie, dearie! To think the Dragon King should be afraid of that! Of its power! Its protection! What's its protection worth so far away from home, too?" He sneers, pointing at the flag.

But as the wretched Joseph and Matilda lay hands on the children, there is a blinding flash and St. George appears, gazing down on them with contempt:

"Unworthy son of your great country," he cries, *"Behold the power at which you scoff. What England holds she guards — her flag means sure protection."*

Terrified, Joseph and Matilda fly into the Dragon Forest.

Meanwhile, the Dragon King has laid his plans well. He lures Betty into the forest with a troupe of elves. Rosamund, finding her missing,

The stage version of "Where the Rainbow Ends" proved to be a magical theatrical experience for many children.

47

goes after her and the two boys follow. Cubby also has taken up the search. The children are lost in the dread Dragon Wood as the sun sets.

Uncle Joseph now makes a terrible discovery — the bottle of Colonial Mixture he has stolen from Cubby has jogged the piece of carpet from his pocket. He can no longer summon the Dragon King. Hyaenas are abroad. They are on Joseph's scent, so he dodges up a tree and lets them pursue Aunt Matilda, reflecting as they devour her that it will save the expense of a funeral. He feels faint with hunger and is mad with thirst. He remembers the Colonial Mixture and takes it from his pocket and drains the bottle. Only then does he look at the label and warning printed at the bottom:

Poison To Traitors

This episode is of course excised from the bowdlerized version which has been published for acting: in that version Uncle Joseph finds the bottle of Colonial Mixture when he first enters St. George's ground, he tastes it and says "Ugh! It tastes awful!"

Meanwhile, Cris and Blunders, searching for the girls, meet a young Englishman. He explains that he also was going to the "Land Where the Rainbow Ends" but got fed up. He has stayed in the Dragon Wood where he is able to live an idle life fishing and eating the Dragon Fruit. He has to pay for this by surrendering his letters from home unopened, and by wearing the Dragon's Badge. In return he is surrounded by Dragon Light which keeps the wild beasts at bay.

"People call me the Slacker," he explains, and jeers at the two boys for wanting to press on. Suddenly, Blunders asks him what the end of it all will be. The Slacker points, and the boys, speechless with horror, see a worm-like creature with a human face and blind eyes, slithering towards the swamps, leaving behind a trail of foul slime. They urge the Slacker to come with them, to start anew.

"How do you know you'll get there?" sneers the Slacker.

Cris sets his teeth: "Well, we shall have done our best," he says.

Blunders joins in: "Of course. Nelson said *England expects that every man shall do his duty*' not *England expects every man to win*'. "

This has an extraordinary effect upon the Slacker. He falls to the ground in fear and the Dragon Light fades. "Stop! Stop!" he cries. "It cannot burn because you have recalled the noble influence of the heroic dead. Leave me, leave me. Would you have me eaten by the beasts?"

Again the boys urge him to act like an Englishman and come with them to Where the Rainbow Ends.

"Come with you?" cries the Slacker, "To fight, to work — perhaps to starve? Never. I'll stay here!"

Immediately the Dragon Light is restored to the craven, who runs off to continue his life of idleness until the dreaded day when he too becomes a hideous worm-like creature.

The boys' horror and shame for their countryman is soon dispelled however, for they find the girls and the joyful Cubby who has been protecting them. All four make their way to the edge of the Dragon Wood, and it is at this moment that the Dragon King strikes, sending his flying dragons to snatch them up and take them to his castle high up on the Thundercloud Mountains where they are beyond the protection of St. George.

The Dragon King enters and sits upon his throne to pronounce judgement on the children:

"You children of England stand guilty to the charge of having dared to place yourselves under the protection of an Ideal, one George of England, Saint and Patron. Know then Ideals are the dragons' greatest enemies, for where ideals are honoured our power is unknown, and this one in particular is here most hated. For he alone can build about your country, England, a sure, impregnable defence — the wall of patriotism, quoting to boy and girl of Crecy, Poitiers, of Waterloo and Trafalgar, and thus inciting valour in each British heart, build on your country's past a great future. Therefore what you have done is a capital offence and the punishment is death!"

49

A sight to gladden the English heart — the flag of St. George flying high from the imposing fortifications at Warwick Castle.

Cubby, however, has other ideas. Like a true British Lion, he is game to the last. He communicates to Rosamund the idea of taking off his red, white and blue ribbons, and from the red ribbon and Cris's handkerchief she makes a flag of England. The boys scale the staff tower and even as the execution party arrives they strike the Dragon Standard and hoist the Red Cross of England.

In a blinding flash of light St. George appears upon the battlements. A thrilling fight ensues in which he slays, once more, the Dragon King. The castle crumbles into dust and the Dragon Soldiers fall headlong into the abyss. St. George points the way down a steep mountain path and the children following it come to the golden beach where their parents await and a ship of England rides out to sea. As they row out to the ship, St. George appears on the helm and the sailors, seeing him, cheer. St. George is returning to England with them: "Not to be lifeless stone in a cold cathedral, but to live henceforth and forever in the hearts of the children of his race".

Where the Rainbow Ends was once an annual play. It is estimated that 20 million people had seen the stage performance by 1961: a natural for television you might say. Why then has it been banished from our stage and from library and bookshop shelves? It is a powerful and potent story. Its influence could only be for good. But it is a book which describes exactly the type of mind and the type of traitor who would censor it. It is easy to see why it is loathed by the education and media establishment of today. It relates, in simple allegorical form, every educational aim normal to any society which has the healthy instinct to survive: honour, courage, integrity and kindliness. It also portrays, in devastating terms, the type of liberalist whose personal littleness, greed and self-interest is expressed in his hatred of his own country. It underscores the vital part in the national life of the past — "of the noble influence of the heroic dead". It holds up to scorn the idler and unenthused, and forecasts the dread end which awaits him.

Those who plan to reduce the nation to a rootless, idle, malleable rabble, would never allow such a book to have any part in the spiritual and cultural formation of succeeding generations. But to their horror, dismay and loathing, the spirit of the book is not dead, nor is the spirit of St. George. It is merely asleep, waiting to be awakened.

CHAPTER SEVEN
Saint George and the Dragon

For most people: "St. George killed a dragon". Those who consider themselves too progressive to believe in such strange fancies look upon him as a vague, shadowy figure, perhaps hardly less legendary than the dragon itself. The dragon stories have been carefully examined by the scholar (another German I'm afraid) J.B. Aufauser, who makes the point that the legend of the dragon did not appear in writing before the 10th century, but that it then appeared all over Europe and the Middle East at about the same time.

H. Delehaye, in his *Legendes Grecques des Saints Militaire* (1909), confirms that the dragon cannot be substantiated from any earlier legends of St. George. Nevertheless, some may feel that the sudden appearance of the story in the literature of so many countries in so short a space of time rules out its spread from a single source and points to a widespread oral tradition.

The familiar version of the story is found in the *Legend Aurea* of James of Voraigne, dating from 1255 AD:

> For some time a terrible dragon had ravaged all the country round the city of Selena in Lybia, making its lair in a swamp. Its breath caused pestilence whenever it approached the town. So the people gave the dragon two sheep every day to satisfy its hunger, but when the sheep were all gone, a human victim was necessary. Lots were drawn to determine the victim and they fell upon the king's daughter. The king offered all his wealth to purchase a substitute, but the people had pledged themselves that no substitute should be allowed. And so the maiden was led, dressed as a bride, to the edge of the marsh. There St. George chanced to ride by on a white horse and asked the maiden what she did. But she bade him leave her, lest he might also perish, but he would not. When the dragon appeared he made the Sign of the Cross and bravely transfixed it with his lance. Then asking the maiden for

her girdle he bound it round the neck of the monster and there-
upon the maiden was able to lead it meek as a lamb. They then
returned to the city where St. George bade the people have no
fear, but only be baptized. The king would have given St. George
half his kingdom, but the Saint replied that he must ride on about
God's business, bidding the king meanwhile to take good care of
God's churches, honour the clergy, and pity the poor.

An obvious comparison is with the story of St. Francis and the Wolf of Gubio, which became popular at about the same time:

> *A fierce wolf made its lair outside the town of Gubio, terrorizing*
> *the citizens and raiding their flocks. One day St. Francis came to*
> *the town. Hearing of the depredations of the wolf he went out to*
> *meet it, in spite of the tearful entreaties of the townsfolk that he*
> *should not risk his life. The wolf came bounding out of its lair to*
> *meet St. Francis, snarling horribly, but St. Francis remained calm*
> *and spoke sternly to it, recounting its misdeeds. The wolf hung his*
> *head in shame and St. Francis promised him that if he amended*
> *his ways the townsfolk would feed him in return for working as a*
> *guardian and watchdog of the town. The wolf held up his paw to*
> *shake hands on the deal. St. Francis led the wolf back into the*
> *town where at first the citizens were filled with terror. St. Francis*
> *told them not to be afraid, and assured them that if they fed the*
> *wolf from their tables he would do them good service in return.*
> *The wolf wagged his tail and frisked about to show his agreement.*
> *St. Francis went on his way and the wolf worked happily for the*
> *townsfolk for many years.*

Both stories are allegories of the same sort. In the dragon story the city represents Man. The king is his reason, which ought to rule the passions. The princess is the soul and her girdle is the middle path of moderation. The dragon is the instincts and passions of the flesh. If the passions are not governed by reason their demands will increase. At first they may be placated with small things, but growing stronger by these concessions they eventually threaten the immortal soul itself. St. George on the white horse symbolizes the Grace of God, which if it is accepted enables the soul to overcome the passions of the flesh, binding them with the girdle — the middle path of moderation. The desires and faculties of the flesh are then brought meek and submissive into their proper service of the whole man.

The story is therefore an allegory of man's destiny, his fall and salvation. The dragons are internal, not external, monsters.

One thing the many dragon stories of the 10th century are agreed upon is that the city of Selena was either in Libya or Egypt. One cannot help thinking that in the descriptions and drawings of dragons from Roman times onward, they look and sound remarkably like Nile crocodiles, though embellished with wings and serpentine tails, and that according to some versions of the dragon story it was *after* St. George had slain the dragon in Egypt that he returned to Nicomedia and defied the Emperor. The crocodile has halitous, pestilential breath and an unpleasant habit of lurking in swamps near to human habitation, the better to snatch children and maidens, and St. George, as we know, served under Diocletian in Egypt.

Which brings us to the myth of Perseus, Andromeda and the sea monster...

Sceptics in high glee point out to us that Perseus was said to have slain the sea monster and saved the maiden, Andromeda, at Jaffa, a few miles from Lydda, St. George's birthplace. Therefore, they declaim, the pagan myth was transferred to St. George. Their argument appears to be this: "As the dragon is a pagan myth, so is St. George". To which our reply is: "We know that the dragon is a myth, but we also know that St. George is real, because he was venerated for centuries before the dragon story appeared".

What the sceptics are in fact saying without realizing it is this: that the Perseus myth was buried deep in the folk-memory for 500 years, from the end of Paganism in the 5th century until the 10th century when, according to them, it suddenly burst out all over the place attached to St. George. Our reply is: "Thank you for the admission that such a thing can happen, we will use it later. Further, have you considered the possibility that Perseus did exist and slew a crocodile which was about to carry off a young woman it had lain in wait for and this is precisely why people told the story for centuries, embroidering it with such symbols as a winged helmet

Representing England's fighting spirit, St. George appears on this war memorial at Lichfield in Staffordshire.

and sandals and changing the crocodile into a serpentine monster? Are you unaware of the persistence of folk-memories for centuries?"

I do not, as a matter of fact, intend to assert that the myth of St. George and the Dragon may have its origins in the possibility of George, when serving in Egypt, rescuing some young woman from a lurking crocodile and slaying the beast. This would be no mean achievement with the weapons of the day, but it is at least as likely that such a memory could lie dormant for 500 years to spring into the light of day wherever St. George was venerated, as that the myth of Perseus could lie dormant for the same 500 years to suddenly emerge and attach itself, for no apparent reason, to St. George. However I do intend to offer an hypothesis which relies upon the possibility

This statue of St. George slaying the dragon can be seen near to Lord's Cricket Ground in London.

of a truth being long dormant and half-remembered but suddenly springing forth clothed in allegory and symbolism. If the sceptics and the sneerers think this is unfair, we need only remind them that they started this sort of "Higher Criticism": they have used it, and they have admitted it!

It has already been suggested that the widespread and simultaneous appearance of the dragon legend in literature indicates a much older oral tradition, a tradition which may rest upon a different sort of fact than that related by the allegory. Readers will also remember that the Roman Emperors used their coinage for propaganda. For example the coinage issued by Octavius Caesar before he assumed the title of "Augustus" depicts him as a just but stern Roman magistrate. In this way he assured the Romans that the Republic was safe in his hands, even though he was Consul for Life. His coinage *after* he became "Emperor" lends him, by a cast of countenance, an aura of divinity. In the same way the image of Britannia on Claudius's coins informed the Empire that he had conquered Britain.

Now we come to a matter of great importance. A coin struck by Constantine shows a fallen dragon surmounted by the Greek initials of the name of Christ. The symbolism is obvious: Christ overcomes the dragon. But what does the dragon symbolize? Today we would unhesitatingly answer "Satan", or "Sin", but dragons, as the banners of Wales and Wessex show, were not always considered Satanic in the ancient world, but merely fearsome, so we must ask the question again — Why a dragon? What does it symbolize?

A clue is provided by the Roman historian, Ammianus Marcellinus, whose Silver Latin was to be recovered to play a notable part in the Renaissance. He describes how the Caesar was recognized in battle by the *purple standard of the dragon*.

In the original story, was the dragon St. George battled with and overcame, Diocletian, Emperor and Dragon-bearer of Rome? Certainly St. George did not overcome the Roman Empire with the sword. By his example which *"when faith by*

A graphic portrayal of the slaying of the dragon is captured on this sign for "The George" inn at Alstonefield, near Leek in Staffordshire.

others was concealed", he inspired many to remain faithful. He overcame the last great assault of the Dragon upon the Church. Through the merits of his martyrdom the Dragon was bound by the Church's girdle and led, meekly as a lamb, into the service of Christ. Was this the buried memory, brought to the surface by monks and scholars in the intellectual ferment of the 10th century, to symbolize the truth of the greatness of St. George?

CHAPTER EIGHT
Pendragons, Knights and Kings

D ragons, as we have said, were not necessarily regarded as evil. They were regarded as fierce, and as such an appropriate badge or banner for the Emperor, whose personal standard, as Ammianus Marcellinus tells us, was the purple dragon. This, incidentally, was not a flag as we know it, but something more like a windsock. "Pen" in the Celtic languages means "Head" or "Chief" — hence "Pendragon" suggests "Emperor".

In 383 AD the legions in Britain proclaimed Magnus Maximus Emperor. If the Welsh legend *Beuddwyd Maxen Wledig* is reliable, this took place at Segontium (Caernarvon) which had replaced in importance the old headquarters of the XXth Valeria Victrix at Chester. Bede tells us that:

> *Maximus, an able and energetic man, well fitted to be Emperor had not ambition led him to break his oath of allegiance, was elected Emperor by the army in Britain almost against his will, and he crossed into Gaul at its head ... the Emperor Valentinian was driven out of Italy ... within a short time, however, he regained the Empire, and trapping Maximus in Aquileia, he captured him and put him to death.*

Maximus, according to the pedigree which was carved on the "Pillar of Eliseg" (still standing, though worn smooth) at Valle Crucis Abbey, became the father-in-law through his daughter Sevira, of the native British king, Vortigern, whose descendants were the Princes of Powys. The Harleian Pedigrees trace the descent of the princes of Dyfed and of the Isle of Man from Maximus.

In the earliest known copy of the "Cantreds and Commotes of Wales", the princes of Glywysing are descended from

59

Caernarvon Castle, Wales. The Roman name for the town was Segontium and, according to Welsh legend, it was here in 383 AD that Magnus Maximus was proclaimed Emperor by the legions in Britain.

Owain, son of Maximus. The Jesus College pedigrees name Constantine III as a son of Maximus and a Northern pedigree shows Octa, ancestor of the Kings of Kent, to be descended from Leo, son of Maximus. The Jesus College pedigrees also name the wife of Maximus as "Elen", daughter of the "King" of Cornwall. It is with this Elen, it is claimed, that St. Helen is often confused. Certainly Elen's name is found in many places in North Wales: *Coed Elen*, the forest beneath Segontium; *Sarn Elen*, the stretch of Roman road once part of the paved way from Segontium to Harlech; and *Dolwydd Elan*, the castle dominating the Lledr where Llewellen ("Lion of Elen") was born.

In 407 AD a Constantine was proclaimed Emperor at Segontium, styling himself "Constantine III". Nennius tells us that a Roman Emperor named Constantine is buried at Segontium, the inscription on his tomb stating that he was the son of one "Great very great", an obvious reference to Magnus Maximus. Bede dismisses him as a common soldier and says that "Once he had obtained power he crossed into Gaul, where he was tricked into many worthless treaties by the barbarians, and caused great harm to the commonwealth".

Bede is no doubt referring to the fact that Constantine III took with him what remained of the field army and probably the best of the garrison troops on the Wall, for he mentions later that Britain had been "robbed of the flower of its young men, who had been led away by rash tyrants and were never to return". There are no "ifs" in history, but it is tempting to speculate what might have happened if first Magnus Maximus and then Constantine III had been content with a Northern Empire.

It is entirely likely that Magnus Maximus would appoint his sons as Counts and Dukes of various parts of his Northern Empire before his ill-fated expedition, and as personal representatives of the Emperor they would fly the Dragon Standard (Gildas refers to Maglocunus of Anglesey as "The Island Dragon"). As central authority in the West broke down, so the

61

offices of Count and Duke
became hereditary and so too
did the Imperial banner. This is
the origin of the Red Dragon of
Wales and the Golden Dragon
of Wessex. It seems probable that
through Owain Glyndwr on the
one hand, and the Saxon princess
Matilda, wife of Henry I (Beauclerc) on
the other, the Royal House of Great Britain is descended from
Magnus Maximus, and not since his proclamation at Segontium has Britain been subordinated to a larger Imperium.

The teasing out of the facts from legends suggests that the
mysterious figures of Uther Pendragon and Arthur ("Duke of
Battles" or "Count of Britain", not "King") were descended
from Magnus Maximus, possibly through Constantine III and
the Ambrosius (Emrys) Aurelius of whom Bede tells us:

> *Their leader at this time was Ambrosius Aurelius, a modest
> man of Roman origin, who was the sole survivor of the catas-
> trophe in which his royal parents had perished. Under his leader-
> ship the Britons took up arms, challenged their conquerors to
> battle, and with God's help inflicted a defeat on them (493 AD).
> Thenceforward victory swung first to one side, and then to the
> other, until their (the Angles) defeat at the battle of Badon Hill,
> when the Britons made a considerable slaughter of them.*

These are the victories which legend accredits to Arthur, so
it seems odd that neither Gildas nor Bede (who relied very
much on Gildas) mentions Arthur, if he really existed. What is
overlooked is the possibility that "Arthur" (and possibly
"Uther" too) were nicknames — "Arthur" is after all the Latin
Artorius ("The Bear"), and although these names were remem-
bered by their troops and passed on in story and legend, we
may be reading about them, in the few scraps of written record
which have survived, under their real names, such as, for
example, Ambrosius Aurelius.

The only *royal* parents a Roman-Briton could have had at the time Bede refers to would be a descendant of Magnus Maximus, and this, together with the title "Pendragon", suggests that Uther and Arthur belonged to the Romano-British establishment of city and villa, rather than to the world of the native *reges* — tribal chiefs recognized by Rome; that they were *Britanni* (Roman citizens) not *Britones* (Celtic tribesmen). In a world returning to barbarism, they stood for *Romanitas* — the Roman Order and Roman Culture. They considered Britain a part of that world — but a sovereign part — which through Magnus Maximus had inherited the authority of the distant and still receding Imperium.

It is in this context that we can see the possibility of the legendary "Knights of the Round Table", readily identifiable as heavy cavalry on the Byzantine model, being, as Revill and Crichton suggest, "The Order of the Society of St. George and the Round Table", with St. George as their ideal and pattern. It seems reasonable that St. George, the illustrious soldier-saint, whose cult had reached Rome within a few decades of his martyrdom, should be chosen as Patron of Rome's last and half-forgotten legion in Britain.

We must also admit that this legend of Arthur and St. George may be a much later embroidering of the legend of the Round Table. At all events it proves once again the affection of Englishmen for St. George and their choice of him as Patron from very early times.

CHAPTER NINE
Saint George,
Patron of England

It is sometimes argued, usually by nit-pickers or those who, like Uncle Joseph in *Where the Rainbow Ends*, just hate anything to do with their own country if it is good and splendid, that St. George is not the Patron Saint of England because he has never been adopted as such! I know of no ceremony or ritual, ecclesiastical or secular, whereby a saint is so adopted, whether by Emperor or Patriarch, Pope or Prince, and we may safely dismiss this quibble. Nevertheless, to finally rout the quibblers, let us look at how the adoption of St. George by England developed (as did the adoption of every other Patron Saint) through "official" channels.

As we have seen, there was great veneration of St. George in Anglo-Saxon times, and churches were dedicated to him. It was, however, the Crusades which made St. George preeminent in England. The *Gesta Francorum* is a sober and objective account of the First Crusade by an unknown knight who took part in that incredible march from Constantinople, around the Mediterranean coast, to Jerusalem. The author tells us that at the Siege of Antioch in 1098 AD the Christian host was hard-pressed, when they saw a vision in the sky of St. George leading knights on white horses and bearing white banners. The author adds simply: "This was true, for many of our men saw it". One immediately thinks of the Angel of Mons, to which thousands of hard-bitten soldiers have testified.

On the eve of his departure for the Holy Land in 1199 AD, Richard I, the Lion Heart, called a Council of the Realm at

King Richard I, the Lion Heart, (left) declared St. George to be his personal patron.

The Feast of St. George, on 23rd April, was first placed in the national calendar by Henry III (right) in 1220.

Winchester, delivering the guidance of the Kingdom into the hands of William Longchamps. Perhaps as a result of the vision recorded in the *Gesta Francorum* he placed himself and his army under the special protection of St. George. He then commanded that his knights should fasten to their knees blue thongs to distinguish the English from the other Crusaders, "by means of which, being minded of their future glory, they might be stirred up to behave themselves valiantly".

At the Siege of Jerusalem, Richard claimed to have seen a vision of St. George bearing a red-cross banner. Although he himself did not enter Jerusalem with the victorious army, declaring himself unworthy to do so, in gratitude for the victory he repaired the church over the grave of St. George at Lydda, and there took the Saint as his personal patron.

In 1220 AD Henry III ordered the Feast of St. George, 23rd April, to be placed in the national calendar. In 1222 AD the Synod of Bishops, meeting at Oxford, decreed that St. George's Day should become a lesser holiday. When Henry's son, Edward I, ascended the throne, he ordered that the Banner of St. George should be borne before the Monarch, joining the

65

King Edward III (left) who, under the patronage of St. George, founded the Order of the Garter in 1345.

James II (right) was a monarch who was devoted to St. George. He even chose 23rd April for his coronation in 1685.

banners of St. Edmund of Canterbury, king and martyr, and St. Edward the Confessor.

Edward III (1327-77 AD) founded the Order of the Garter in 1345 AD under the patronage of St. George, who was named "Specyel protectour and defendour of this royaume". In 1386 Richard II ordered his soldiers to "Bere a signe of the armes of St. George, large, bothe before and behynde". In 1399 Archbishop Arundel called a Synod at St. Paul's to receive a petition from the clergy which read: *"The feast of St. George the Martyr, who is the spiritual patron of the soldiery of England, should be appointed to be solemnized throughout England and observed as a holiday, even as other nations observe the feast of their own patron".*

It was at the Siege of Harfleur that Henry V rallied his soldiers with the great battle-cry immortalized by Shakespeare:

"God for Harry, England and St. George!"

and in that year Archbishop Chichele had St. George's Day raised to one of the principal feasts in the English Calendar, with an entire day's holiday being universally observed.

There is a contemporary account of the Battle of Agincourt, which Shakespeare seems to have relied upon, which tells us:

> And then every Englishman knelt down and put a little portion of earth into his mouth, and then said the King in a high voice, "In the name of Almighty God and of St. George, advance the banner, and St. George this day them help!" Then the two battle lines met together and fought hard a long time, but Almighty God and St. George fought that day for us and granted our King the victory.

Great celebrations were held by the court at Windsor every St. George's Day, beginning with the solemn procession of the Knights of the Garter to St. George's Chapel, followed by jousts and feasting, and these were emulated in every town and village throughout the country. The Reformation did not change the devotion of the people to St. George, and Henry VIII decreed that St. George's Day, along with Our Lady's Days and those of the Apostle Evangelists should be kept as holy days.

The Puritans of the "Commonwealth" government banned not only holy days, but even mince pies! Christmas Day, they ordered, should be observed with gloom and penitence. The celebration of St. George's Day did not survive this period and in spite of the efforts of Charles II, never fully recovered.

Charles II and his brother, the Duke of York, later James II, both shared a devotion to St. George, James II choosing St. George's Day, 1685, for his coronation. James II was one of our greatest admirals. He invented the manoeuvre of "fighting in line" which was to serve the Royal Navy well up to the Battle of the River Plate in 1939. It was he who gave the Navy its Royal Ensign of the Cross of St. George, with, in the dexter canton, the Union Jack.

After James II there was a further decline in veneration of St. George until the 18th century, when we had four King Georges in succession. The long reign of the much-loved George III saw a revival of town and village celebrations. However the Agricultural and Industrial Revolutions disrupted rural life, displacing hundreds of thousands of country folk into

67

An annual event in the calendar of the Boy Scout and Girl Guide Movement is the St. George's Day parade. This one is taking place at Alton, Hampshire.

the grim and cheerless industrial towns where there was little inclination, and no holidays, to celebrate anything. This was the situation lamented by the little girl who grew up to write *Where the Rainbow Ends.*

The founding at the beginning of the century, by Baden Powell, of the Scout and Guide Movement with St. George as their exemplar, and their annual St. George's Day parades, has done something to redress the balance, as has the founding, under Her Majesty's patronage, of the Royal Society of Saint George. The Royal Society some years ago presented a banner of St. George to the Greek Orthodox Church at Lydda which incorporates the foundations and some of the fabric of the original church built by Constantine.

In the first week of December, 1917, General Allenby had advanced within sight of Jerusalem. There he halted his forces and was torn by a great dilemma. How could he order his guns to fire upon the Holy City? Yet he could not leave a fortified city in his rear. For three days he pondered what to do. On the

Colonel T. E. Lawrence ("Lawrence of Arabia") who accompanied General Allenby and the British Army when they marched into Jerusalem under the flag of St. George in December 1917.

third day, knowing that he must make a decision soon, he spent the night in prayer in his tent. Finally resolved that he must order the attack, he was called out from his tent at dawn. Three Turkish officers under a flag of truce had approached the British lines. They informed General Allenby that their commander had declared Jerusalem an "Open City". The Turks would withdraw and the British advance without any exchange of fire.

It transpired that during the night the Turkish commander had been reading and had come across an ancient prophecy that Jerusalem would be taken from the Turks by "Allah Nebi", "God's Prophet". The Turkish Commander had immediately realized the significance of his opponent's name — General Allenby — and had determined to surrender the city.

On 9th December, as the Turks withdrew, the British Army marched in open order toward the city gates, led by General Allenby, accompanied by Colonel T.E. Lawrence, on horseback, and preceded by the Banner of St. George and of England, now incorporated into the Union Flag of Great Britain. At the gates of the Holy City, General Allenby dismounted and removed his cap, as did the members of his staff. They entered Jerusalem and walked bare-headed through the streets to the

Church of the Holy Sepulchre, where they knelt and prayed. Thus, finally, did the Banner of St. George lead the Crusader Army of England into Jerusalem.

Mention has been made of St. Edmund of Canterbury and St. Edward the Confessor. Whenever there is a proposal for greater celebration, public or private, of St. George's Day, it seems that there is always someone to chirrup, "But St. George wasn't English. Why don't we celebrate the Feast Days of St. Edmund or St. Edward and make one of them our Patron Saint?"

Experience shows that generally two sorts of people take this line. The first are those who feel that they have been diminished by not being the one to think of something first. Unless they are sticking their oar in and having their pennyworth they do not believe they exist. The second sort have more sinister motives. They do not want the English to celebrate *any* day and they use an old trick of the Marxist cadre to cause argument and create division. They are skilled at countering any suggestion which they identify as inimical to their policies, by proposing an alternative. They know that they can leave the rest to the first sort of person, who will immediately seek to validate their existence by proposing another, another, and yet another alternative. The result is confusion and disunity; they call it "dialecticizing" the situation.

Enough has been said of the development of the veneration of St. George in England to establish, beyond fatuous dispute, that he *is* the Patron Saint of England. Nevertheless both St. Edmund of Canterbury, king and martyr, and St. Edward the Confessor, have their place. St. Edmund is the Patron of the English *race*, that is of the English race as a whole and of all Englishmen and women wherever they may dwell. St. Edward the Confessor is the Personal Patron of the English Monarch. St. George is the Patron Saint of England, that is of all who dwell within her bounds, who taste her salt and who have their bread from her bounty.

St. George's Day is England's Day

70

CHAPTER TEN
A Day of Adornment

Pope Pius XII, in his *Summi Pontifacatus* of 20th October, 1939, had this to say:

> *"It is well to insist here that this sense of universal brotherhood which Christian teaching awakens and keeps alive in our minds is not opposed to the love of a man's country and for the glorious memories it has for him. This same Christian teaching assures us that God has established an order of charity which binds us to love better and to cherish more those who are bound to us by special ties."*

This was a theme to which Pius XII was to return constantly during his pontificate. As at the beginning, so too near its close, he spoke again of a true Christian Nationalism: this time it was in an address to a gathering of poets (21st October, 1957). Pius spoke to them of the close communications now existing between countries: but not in order to repeat the conventional wisdom of "Peace, Progress, Prosperity", rather to warn of the danger that nations could weaken in their national traditions and renounce their native customs:

> *"Any kind of cosmopolitanism which would cause the nations to renounce their national characteristics must be avoided."*

G.K. Chesterton had put the matter succinctly many years before: *"The Patriot loves his Patria, but the cosmopolitan does not love the Cosmos".*

Why should Pius XII return, as he so often did, to a theme which the one-worlders assure us is "old-fashioned", "out of date", at variance with the "New World Order"? The answer is that patriotism is a *natural virtue*. It is part of what theology terms *Pietas*. We are required by Natural Justice to love the land

G.K. Chesterton (1874-1936), one of England's literary masters.

of our birth, but as Christians we are commanded to do so by the Commandment "Honour thy father and thy mother". Patriotism is but an extension of the filial piety imposed upon us by the Commandments.

A people who, because of a tradition and ancient heritage that they share in common, feel that they are one, and different from other peoples, and who are prepared to shed their blood to defend that unity, are a nation. Their culture is, as it were, the body of the nation, ordering and continuing their existence through time; the proxy of the dead and the enfranchisement of the unborn.

Before Christianity created the nations of Europe and sanctified patriotism, even pagans knew that it was a natural virtue. For the Greeks no crime was worse than treason. The corpse of the traitor was not permitted to pollute the sacred soil of the homeland but was cast into the sea.

Rupert Brooke, whose famous poem "The Soldier" embodies the brave and noble English spirit.

For the Greek no penalty was considered so severe as banishment. There is an inscription upon the tomb of a Greek buried in a foreign land — "Far from my own land I lie, and more bitter is that to me than death itself", and for Odysseus the very smoke of home was brighter than the flames of a foreign fire.

Rupert Brooke, fortified with the English spirit, took comfort in another thought:

> *If I should die, think only this of me:*
> *That there's some corner of a foreign field*
> *That is for ever England. There shall be*
> *In that rich earth a richer dust concealed.*

(The Soldier)

As with the pagans, so too with Christian saints. St. Columcille, as he left Ireland, said "There will be no night — I will
not hide it — that a tear will not come into my eye". Robert
Browning understood well what Columcille meant in his own
longing for England, expressed with characteristic English
understatement:

> *Oh, to be in England*
> *Now that April's there,*
> *And whoever wakes in England*
> *Sees, some morning, unaware,*
> *That the lowest boughs and the brush-wood sheaf*
> *Round the elm-tree bole are in tiny leaf,*
> *While the chaffinch sings on the orchard bough*
> *In England — now!*
>
> (Home Thoughts from Abroad)

For the patriot, the decay of his country, contrasted with its
true spirit, is a heartache, never expressed better than in the
words Shakespeare placed in the mouth of the aged John of
Gaunt:

> *This royal throne of kings, this sceptered isle,*
> *This earth of majesty, this seat of Mars,*
> *This other Eden, demi-Paradise;*
> *This fortress built by Nature for herself*
> *Against infection and the hand of war;*
> *This happy breed of men, this little world;*
> *This precious stone set in the silver sea,*
> *Which serves it in the office of a wall,*
> *Or as a moat defensive to a house,*
> *Against the envy of less happier lands;*
> *This blessed plot, this earth, this realm, this England.*
>
> (Richard II)

To reject the duties of patriotism is to reject, to a greater or

Fluttering in the Cotswold breeze, the flag of St. George is flown from the tower of Great Rissington church in Gloucestershire.

lesser extent, the Will of God, for God has willed that one be born in one country rather than another, and He has therefore provided in our native land the most abundant means for our perfection and salvation. However, love grows outward, from our family to our neighbourhood, to our country, and when we think of England it is not perhaps of the whole country, but of our native spot, or of some happening long ago, of something that brought our heart with it, or of those ever dearest to us. It is not strange, surely, that according to the measure of our affection for our small native place, so will be our affection for that greater place which is our native land.

For Charles Kingsley, a great Englishman, nothing could be dearer than his own portion of England. For him, the fields and hedgerows, neat homesteads and village spires of the well-ordered countryside, were as lovely as the grandeur of the wildest mountains:

> Give me Bramshill Common
> (St. John's Harriers by)
> Or the vale of Windsor,
> England's golden eye.
> Show me life and progress
> Beauty, health and man;
> Houses fair, trim gardens
> Turn where'er I can
>
> (The Invitation to Tom Hughes)

For Hilaire Belloc, the despoliation of the English landscape was a source of continual sorrow, expressed in his lament:

> Spirits that call and no-one answers;
> Ha'nacker's down and England's done.
> Wind and thistle for pipe and dancers
> And never a ploughman under the sun,
> Never a ploughman. Never a one.
>
> (Ha'nacker Mill)

To say "The world is everyone's" is to say very little, for if board and hearth are public to all, we are left without a home and are born and live in an inn. Those who proclaim themselves "Internationalists" and say that no country has a claim on them are saying that they belong to no country and no country can trust them. Worse than these are they who say *"ubi bene ibi patria"* — "Where I prosper, there is my Fatherland". That cry is louder today than ever before, boldly embraced by those who sing the sirens' song of "trade" and "prosperity" to be had through a single currency and a Federal Europe. The words of the Scots patriot, Fletcher of Saltoun, put the matter in perspective:

> *Show me a bombast and a braggart, and I will show you a knave and a scoundrel, but show me a Patriot who loves his country, and I will show you a true lover of humanity. Show me a man who says that he loves all nations equally with his own, and I will show you a man who lacks all discernment, and loves none but himself.*

Of Fletcher it was written: "He would gladly die for his country, but he would not do a base thing to save it".

Naturally this love of our homeland will not be on a high note during all our waking lives, for there is a rhythm in affection as in everything else. Our love of our homeland has its focal points, and Christianity in its centuries-old wisdom has provided for this with the custom of Patron Saints. The feast day of our Patron Saint ought to be a day of rejoicing and fellowship, and the love for our neighbours beyond our borders will depend for its strength on the vigour of our love for our own kind.

Chesterton, in one of his most important books, *Orthodoxy*, says that *"If a man should love his country his country will adorn itself for him, as a woman adorns herself when she is loved"*. St. George's Day is England's Day. Let us make it a Day of Adornment.

CHAPTER ELEVEN
Banners and Roses

We owe most of our knowledge of the transfer of St. George's body to Lydda, to Theodosius, Bishop of Jerusalem, who, like Theodotus of Ancyra, relied heavily on Pasicrates. Theodosius tells us that George's friends planted a rose-bush on his grave, and the rose has ever after been associated with St. George and, through him, with England.

The ancient texts say that the rose planted on the grave was the "Rose of Sharon". The plant which we call the "Rose of Sharon" however is not a rose, it is *Hypericum Calycinum*. This is not to say that mention in the ancient texts of the "Rose of Sharon" does not refer to a plant of the genus *Rosa*, and the obvious candidate in that case is *Rosa Damascena*, the Damask Rose, which grew abundantly in Syria and Palestine. At all events the Crusaders took it for granted that the Damask Rose was the one planted on St. George's grave. They brought a great many specimens back to Europe, where it became popular because of its second-flowering habit. It is from this rose that attar of roses and rose-water are made.

Rosa Damascena, however, is not the "Red Rose of England" — that honour goes to the deep red, purplish, *Rosa Gallica Officinalis*, which is also the Red Rose of Lancashire. The Rose represented in English heraldry is neither *Damascena* nor *Gallica*, but a stylized form of the rose of the English hedgerows, the dog-rose. So perhaps it is this, *Rosa Canina*, with its delicate, heart-hurting beauty, which is the true rose of England.

Edward I appears to have been the first English king to

Henry VII, the monarch who created the Tudor Rose which united the Red Rose of Lancaster and the White Rose of York.

choose a rose as his badge, but this was a golden rose. His brother, Edmund Crouchback, the first Duke of Lancaster, "differenced" this by tincturing it red. The White Rose of York (*Rosa Alba Semi-Plena*) was probably also a "differencing" of Edward I's golden rose, inherited by the House of York from the Mortimers through whom they claimed seniority of succession to Richard II. The red and white roses were united by Henry VII in the Tudor Rose, a red rose "charged" upon a white rose, or vice-versa. It is the Tudor Rose with stem and "leaves proper" (that is "natural" not "stylized", and coloured green) which is the Royal Badge of England.

A new twist in the story of the Rose and England is the adoption by the Labour Party of a red rose as its symbol. This has led to the publication in the press, usually just before St. George's Day, of letters to the effect: "As Labour have hijacked the Red Rose of England, I can no longer wear one on St. George's Day, lest I be mistaken for a Labour supporter". It is not known if these letters come from genuine, if slightly stupid, patriots, intent on shooting themselves in the foot, or, as there is some reason to suppose, from persons who sense a revival of Englishness to be contrary to their own objectives and who resort to subtle sabotage. At all events, has anyone ever seen people walking around with red roses in their lapels on every day of the year save St. George's Day, proclaiming their loyalty to the Labour Party? Of course not! Labour supporters wear their red roses at their Party Conference in

The splendid sight of the Union Jack flying high. Here it flies above The Queen's Hotel in Cheltenham, Gloucestershire.

October and nowhere else. If, however, several million Labour voters all decide to wear red roses on St. George's Day, should not all English patriots be delighted?

There is a very simple way for anyone to "difference" their red roses from that of Labour. Let us recall the blue thongs which Richard the Lion Heart commanded his English knights to wear to "difference" themselves from his Norman, Breton and Gascon knights, and which became the blue ribbon of the Garter. Very well then, if anyone is fearful that they might be identified as a Labour Party supporter by wearing a red rose on St. George's Day, they need only tie a blue ribbon to the stem to demonstrate that they are wearing their red rose for England!

None of the shrub or specie roses bloom in April, so what rose should we wear to mark and celebrate our National Day? The answer is not as difficult as the quibblers and nay-sayers would like to make it. We call our national emblem "The Red Rose of England", and that is what we should wear — a red rose of whatever variety it may be.

* * * * * * * *

The flag of the United Kingdom is the Union Jack, and this takes precedence over all other flags, whether national, municipal or "house" flags. No flag may be flown on a public building or from an "official" staff in the United Kingdom without the Union Jack also being flown at an equal or greater height. In the same way, no flag may be paraded in advance of the Union Jack. In Great Britain we leave this to courtesy and good manners, though in some countries, the United States and France for example, it is an offence to fly or parade a foreign flag without the national flag being flown or paraded in the superior position. An offender is quite likely to find himself in prison, if only for protective custody!

The only exception to the rule that the Union Jack must be flown alongside any other flag is in the case of flags flown from cathedrals and parish churches in the provinces of Canterbury and York. The Earl Marshal's warrant, dated 9th February, 1938, stipulates for churches: "A flag of St. George with, in the first quarter, an escutcheon of the arms of the see in which the church is situated". It would be in the spirit of this stipulation for churches of other denominations to fly the Cross of St. George on April 23rd.

In 1962 Her Majesty commanded that all public buildings in England (that is Government offices, Armed Services establishments, Customs Houses, Post Offices, Town and County Halls, etc.) should fly the Union Jack on St. George's Day, and this is the present position.

So far as private persons are concerned there appears to be no reason why they should not, on St. George's Day, fly or display on their private premises, the Banner of England rather than the Union Jack. However, Englishmen resident abroad should not fly or display the Cross of St. George without flying, in courtesy, the flag of their host country. This, of course, applies equally to foreigners living in England who wish to fly their own nation's flag, for whatever reason. They ought, in courtesy, to also fly the Union Jack. And perhaps it is time, as in other countries, that they were required to do so.

CHAPTER TWELVE
Saint George and the Noble Order of the Garter

No consideration of St. George's influence upon England would be complete without mention of the Noble Order of the Garter. We may first of all dispose of the somewhat prurient story that Edward III was inspired to name his new Order of Chivalry by an incident at a court ball when the Countess of Salisbury dropped her garter and Edward, picking it up, exclaimed *"Honi Soit Qui Mal Y Pense"* — "Evil be to him who evil thinks". The "garter" was originally the leather sword-belt with which a knight was invested, and from which we still get the term "A belted earl". The heraldic garter is defined as: "A strap or riband fastened with a buckle so as to form a circle, and having the end pendent".

We must also, however regretfully, reject the suggestion that there was continuity between the legendary "Knights of the Round Table" and Edward's new Order. It is true that Edward III modelled his Order upon the ideas of chivalry which the contemporary French romances, popular at the time, attributed to Arthur and the "Knights of the Round Table". It is also probably true that the "blue thongs" Richard the Lion Heart had ordered his English knights to wear, to distinguish them from other Crusaders, were adopted by Edward as the "garter" to be worn below the left knee of knights of the "Most Honourable Order of Chivalry in Europe".

Whilst the Noble Order of the Garter is considered the premier order of knighthood, it is not the oldest surviving order. That distinction belongs to the "Sovereign and Military Order

King Arthur's Round Table which is currently housed in Winchester's Great Hall, dates from the 16th century. Close inspection reveals that King Arthur's portrait bears more than a passing resemblance to Henry VIII.

of the Knights Hospitallers of St. John of Jerusalem, Rhodes and Malta" which dates back to 1200 AD and the embassies of which, in Malta and Rome, enjoy extra-territorial status.

A connecting link between Richard and Edward III is the Council of the Realm held at Winchester by Edward I before his departure to the Holy Land in which his leading knights assembled in the Great Hall. Here Edward I gave order that the great round table there be encircled with an iron band for its better preservation.

The present Round Table, kept in the gable of the Great Hall is, we must admit, a Tudor fake. Seventeen feet in diameter, the decoration and jointing of the timber-work are plainly Tudor, and it is difficult to understand why anyone should ever have thought it was anything else. The image of "King Arthur" looks remarkably like Henry VIII! Nevertheless there are earlier references to the table. As we have seen, Edward I ordered its repair some 300 years before the Tudors. However old the original table at Winchester, it could not have survived the vicissitudes of seven centuries. It is equally unlikely that Henry VIII could have led his court into the Great Hall and shown them a table they could all plainly see was brand new and which they knew perfectly well had not been there a month before, and say "This is King Arthur's Round Table, it has been here always".

A more probable explanation is that the present table was a replacement, and declared to be a replacement, of an earlier table which had become, despite Edward I's "iron band", decrepit with age. At all events, the romantic notions of Arthur and his "Order of the Round Table" being popularized at the time played their part in the shaping of Edward III's Order of the Garter.

The Order of the Garter as instituted by Edward III included canons and other Church dignitaries, and also poor knights pensioners who were to be maintained at Windsor. Every Companion of the Order of St. George was enjoined to wear his mantle from the first vespers on St. George's Eve until the second vespers on the morrow, wheresoever he might be, whether in the country or without. Edward issued orders that the Feast of his new Fraternity should be celebrated every year at Windsor Castle on St. George's Day. The Order of the Garter originally included ladies who were known as "Dames de la confraternité de St. George".

The chapel of the Order dedicated to St. George was, by Clement VI's Bull of 1348, declared a "Free Chapel", that is free of Papal control and jurisdiction. Two years later, on 23rd

Crowds turn out to witness the splendour and majestic progress of the Garter procession at Windsor Castle in Berkshire.

April, 1350, at the altar of the newly-built chapel of the Order, 25 knights, headed by their sovereign, offered their arms to God and dedicated themselves to His service.

Henry VII and Henry VIII were great supporters of the Order which had undergone few changes in costume or organization since Edward III's time, and the replacement (or invention) of the Winchester Round Table may have been inspired by this. Henry VIII was, of course, known for his love of, and skill at, jousting.

Charles I was the "Great increaser of the honour and renown of this most illustrious Order" and studied every detail of the methods attributed to Arthur, as they were understood by Edward III, for inculcating courtesy and good manners.

The garter was originally light blue silk, with the motto set in pearls, rubies and diamonds. George I changed this for a dark blue velvet garter about an inch wide, edged, buckled and adorned with gold, the motto being set in letters of gold. The collar is gold, and consists of 26 garters each encircling a red rose, enamelled in colour, alternating with interlaced knots, though fewer pieces may be depicted in heraldic representation.

The badge which hangs from the collar (known as "The George") depicts St. George in Roman-type armour, on horseback, slaying the dragon. The Star is eight-pointed, of chipped silver, gold and enamel, and displays the Red Cross of St. George, surrounded by the garter with the motto of the Order. The "Lesser George" is of plain gold and depicts St. George in more mediaeval (or Byzantine) chain mail, on horseback and slaying the dragon. It is worn from the riband of garter blue, four inches wide, which passes over the left shoulder, the gold badge resting on the right hip. The Star and Lesser George are never worn with the collar. The mantle has on the shoulder the badge of the Order, namely a velvet escutcheon charged with the Red Cross of St. George and encircled with the garter and motto. The oath taken when a knight is invested is:

> *"You being chosen to be one of the Honourable Company of the most Noble Order of the Garter shall promise and swear by the Holy Evangelists, by you here touched, that wittingly and will-*

ingly you shall not break any statute of the said Order, or any article in them contained, the same being agreeable and not repugnant to the laws of this Realm and the laws of Almighty God, as far forth as to you belongeth and appertaineth, so help you God and His Holy Word."

One must ponder upon how Euro-federalists and other demeaners of the Queen's sovereignty in the Realm of Great Britain stand in regard to this oath!

Dean Baillie in his Foreword to *St. George's Chapel*, writes:

I think the most romantic thing of all is the great sword which hangs huge and stark behind the altar in the Ambulatory. The sword of Edward III, the man who stood at the moment in English history when Saxons, Normans and Danes became Englishmen in the strenuous efforts of his wars; the man who founded the Order to which the Chapel belongs, and left his mark on English thought and purpose in the ideal of chivalry which he enshrined in the whole foundation.

In 1992 tragedy struck at the very heart of England's heritage and traditions with the great fire which destroyed much of Windsor Castle. The worst victim of the fire was the magnificent 185 foot long St. George's Hall, scene of the most important State banquets, its vaulted ceiling blazoned with the arms of the Knights of the Garter. Happily, all has been fully restored, using photographs from the Royal Collection and computer-generated three-dimensional models. St. George's Hall is now more magnificent than ever, with, instead of the original low-pitched plaster ceiling painted to look like wood, a high-pitched vaulted mediaeval hammer-beam roof. Three hundred English oaks were used to build the roof, reviving joinery and vaulting skills not used for more than four centuries. Seven hundred panels are blazoned with the arms of the Knights of the Garter. The Royal private chapel at one end of the hall has now been redesigned as an ante-chamber to the hall, and the new, resited chapel, has six stained glass windows designed by His Royal Highness the Duke of Edinburgh, and an altar made by Her Majesty the Queen's nephew, Viscount Linley. Once again England and St. George have risen from the flames, and triumphed over disaster.

CHAPTER THIRTEEN
Hurrah for Tom Brown!

Most of us, I imagine, grew up on public school stories, whether they were classics, like Tom Hughes's *Tom Brown's Schooldays*, or the *Wizard's* long-running serial "Smith of the Lower Third". One thing which we probably noticed, without paying it a great deal of attention at the time, was that the schools featured in the stories were organized into Houses. First there was "School House", the oldest and original house. "School House", however, was not the *only* House in the school, nor was it the *whole* school, nor was it the *boss* House. There were other Houses, added as the centuries went by, and these too, under their housemasters, had their honour, their traditions, their pride and indeed their healthy rivalry, played out not only in inter-house football and cricket matches, but in the desire to achieve the best in all fields of school life. "School House" was, nevertheless, the *First among Equals*, it held a Primacy of Honour among the other Houses, as an Archbishop has the Primacy of Honour among his bishops.

Now the simple historical fact is that in the School of Life we call Great Britain — where we were born, where the love that has shaped our hearts and the traditions which have shaped our minds are our heritage from the great dead which we must bequeath to those yet to be born — England *is* "School House". That does not mean that it is the *only* House in Great Britain; it does not mean that it is the *whole* school, or that it must absorb, and is destined to absorb, the other Houses. The simple historical truth is that England is "School House", the First among Equals.

In the first film version of Shakespeare's "Henry V" (1944), Laurence Olivier played the title role. Few can forget the closing lines of his rallying cry to the English troops as they prepare for battle: "Cry God for Harry! England and St. George!"

There are also the other Houses, equal in honour, each with their own traditions and special values, each with their own pride, and all in healthy rivalry for excellence in all fields. There is "Scotland House", "Wales House", "Ulster House", and two which we often overlook: "Manx House" and "Normandy House". Often even more forgotten, are the "Mission Schools" which Great Britain, like the public schools, has planted in places once deserts of knowledge and truth, once wastelands of the civilizing virtues, once bereft of industry and prosperity.

The continuance and cultivation of the special traditions and values of each of these Houses in no way weakens the unity of the whole "School". Let them clash on the association and rugby football fields, let them compete on the cricket field, let them strive mightily to surpass each other in scholarship, science and the arts, and in honour and virtue … they will yet field a single team when the honour of the School requires it.

What can we do in these times of decadence and retreat to cultivate the heritage, which we received freely and without payment on our part? Anyone can sit down and draw up grand plans of salvation, like Hitler in his bunker moving around divisions which had ceased to exist. It is to no purpose to spend time enlisting the aid of forces which we do not command. It is far more difficult to say: "Initiative and action begin with *me*".

There is one thing that every Englishman or woman *can* do. They can begin by saying, in the Spirit of St. George facing the dragon:

> *I am only One,*
> *I can only do what One can do,*
> *But what One can do,*
> *That I will do.*

APPENDIX ONE

The Saint George's Day Association

"For evil to triumph, it is only necessary that good men do nothing."

Edmund Burke (1729-1797)

The St. George's Day Association is an informal gathering of patriotic Englishmen and Englishwomen. There is no "Executive Committee", no membership list, no subscriptions. It does not even have a "membership", it has "associates". Anyone may associate simply by accepting the personal responsibility of observing and celebrating St. George's Day. The minimum responsibility is to wear a rose and fly the flag each April 23rd. It is not intended as a rival organization to the Royal Society of St. George, which has far wider purposes. The "St. George's Day Association" is, if you like, a "commando group" or, better still, a number of "commando groups" spread throughout England. Its watchword is "personal initiative".

Those who wish to do more than wear a rose, but are diffident about publicity, can still invite neighbours round for a toast to England and *"A Happy St. George's Day"*. Some associates organize a St. George's Day dinner or party with friends and relatives.

More "public" action is to write, well in advance of the day, to local newspapers, suggesting that their readers celebrate St. George's Day by wearing a rose, flying the flag, or having a party. Some associates make a point of writing to the Chief Executive of their District or County Council with a reminder that it is Her Majesty's command that the Union Jack be flown from the town hall, county hall, council offices etc. on St. George's Day. Equally useful, in these days of "Pink parsons" and "Pop priests" are letters to local clergy drawing their attention to the Earl Marshal's Warrant, mentioned above. With "desk-top publishing" available, anyone with a computer can design and print half-a-dozen copies of a small poster with a slogan such as

"St. George's Day is England's Day
Wear Your Rose on April 23rd"

and take them round the local shops (especially the florists) to have them displayed at moderate cost. Some of the more determined associates write letters, calling for action, to the Pursuivants of Arms when they find foreign flags being flown alone and without the Union Jack being flown in courtesy. The address is: The Pursuivants of Arms, College of Arms, Queen Victoria Street, London.

Once one starts these initiatives one will become aware of the enthusiasm and good feeling they generate among ordinary English folk. What is sorely needed however are independent "St. George's Day Associations" in every city, town and county to carry out these initiatives. An Association needs no more than two or three associates, and anyone with an ounce of patriotism can start one with a couple of friends or family members. A professional-looking letter-head for writing to the local press can easily be produced by anyone with a computer. Most important, as we shall see, are letters or press releases to local radio stations.

It would be a wonderful thing for England if all readers of this little book and of *This England* were to take up this patriotic task in time for the next St. George's Day.

APPENDIX TWO

Saint George's Day and the BBC

For St. George's Day 1996, all BBC local radio stations, together with Radios 1, 2, 3, 4 and 5, and all four TV channels, were circularised in February by the St. George's Day Association, urging them to offer special programmes for St. George's Day. They were circularised again in March with a "Briefing" — "St. George the Obscure". The response from BBC 2, signed by "Michael Jackson", was plainly unhelpful: "I think it unlikely we will be able to mark the anniversary but we'll certainly look into the possibilities".

The response from the BBC's "Viewer and Listener Information" department pleaded that whereas the Irish, Scots and Welsh celebrated their Patron's days, the English did not, and that they therefore had nothing to report on. This, frankly, is an untruth. Each St. George's Day the Knights of the Garter process at Windsor Castle — a colourful sight. Her Majesty the Queen distributes roses to the Lancashire and Yorkshire Regiment. The cricket season opens with the University match. I name but three — are these events unnewsworthy?

A further letter suggesting that presenters wore a red rose on the day brought the brief response: "I have noted your further comments and suggestions and assure you they will be passed on to those directly concerned". Granada TV pleaded that they were tied to existing schedules, and a further suggestion that the wearing of a rose by presenters would not affect any schedule was turned down with the argument that they could then not refuse to wear all manner of other badges. This of course is nonsense, and does not appear to prevent the shamrock being worn on St. Patrick's Day!

Radio was a different matter. BBC Radio 2 responded with the information that the day would be covered with Judi Spiers presenting her programme from Shakespeare's re-created

Globe Theatre. On 22nd April, the Honorary Secretary of the St. George's Day Association was interviewed for 20 minutes on BBC Radio Sheffield and was able to advocate the celebration of the day. On St. George's Day itself he was interviewed "on line" from BBC Merseyside by BBC local radio stations, Norfolk, Devon, York, Newcastle, Stoke and also on *Late Night North*. He was interviewed "live" on Radio Merseyside. Unfortunately he was unable to fit Radio Derby and Radio Jersey into this busy schedule. The interviews ranged from sympathetic to enthusiastic and a number of the interviewers announced that they had received St. George's Day cards.

During these interviews the Hon. Sec. was able to nail the untruth that St. George had "been abolished" by the Church. The facts are simple: St. George's Day remains unchanged in the Calendar of the Church of England. In the reorganized Calendar of the Roman Catholic Church his Feast Day has, exactly like St. Patrick's Day, St. David's Day, and many other feast days, been designated a Commemoration. This simply means that the liturgy for their feasts need only be used in the countries of which they are Patrons, and not, as in the old Calendar, in every part of the world. He was also able to dispose of the old chestnut about the Red Rose having become the property of the Labour Party. The argument that roses do not bloom in April was countered with the suggestion that artificial roses could be sold for charity. Some interviewers waxed enthusiastic about this, with one calling for "anyone out there" to take up the idea.

The lesson to be learned from this is a simple one — whilst TV producers are plainly hostile to England and to St. George's Day, those on local radio are not, and will be willing to promote celebration of the day if given the right lead. All of the local radio stations mentioned above asked for a local representative to come along for interview. In the very nature of the Association it was not possible to advise them of names and addresses of associates in their broadcasting area.

How different it would be if there were St. George's Day Associations throughout the country, all writing early in the year to their local BBC (and Commercial) radio stations, asking them to arrange special programmes for the day. An Association of even two or three persons could prepare one of their number for an interview. We can make St. George and England meaningful to ourselves and our fellow countrymen if we are willing to make even a small effort.

NOTES

Chapter Two: Since completing the Ms. for this book I have been fortunate to obtain a copy of a scholarly article, *St. George*, by Herbert Thurston, S.J., published in *The Month*, Vol. LXXIV of April, 1892. Thurston records that Gibbon's assertions concerning St. George were refuted at the time by Dr. Milner, a Fellow of the Society of Antiquaries, in an essay, *Historical and Critical Inquiry into the Existence and Character of St. George* (1792) addressed to George, Earl of Leicester. In Thurston's words, Dr. Milner, "confuted with entire success the disingenuous citation of authorities by which Gibbon had sought to identify the martyr-hero, whom all Christendom venerated, with the base and heretical Archbishop of Alexandria ... There was not, he rightly urged, the slightest reliable evidence for this confusion."

Chapter Three: It was only when reading the proofs for this book that I was struck by a fact which, so far as I know, no historian has commented upon. The British "Emperor" Carausius is the only one of the many who took Imperial power, whether in Rome or Constantinople or in one of the provinces, who was a sailor. Rome regarded the Navy as very much the "junior service"; sailors received less pay than their equivalent ranks in the legions. Emperors depended upon the legions for their elevation and continuance in power, and were usually *legates*, i.e. generals, themselves. Carausius, however, was what we term an Admiral and he realized fully the importance of sea power to the security and prosperity of his new Imperium of Great Britain. Is it from Carausius that Britain dates its appreciation of the vital importance of pre-eminence on the sea?

Chapter Four: The English translations of Pasicrates' *Life* of St. George and of the *Encomiums* of Theodosius of Jerusalem and Theodotus of Ancyra are given in *George of Lydda, The Patron Saint of England* by Sir E.A.W. Budge, 1930. The English translations of the apocryphal Coptic (Ethiopic) texts are given in *St. George of Cappadocia* edited by E. Wallis Budge, London 1888.

Chapter Seven: The article by Thurston referred to above supports my suggestion that the "dragon" whom St. George overcame was originally the Emperor Diocletian in particular and the Roman Empire in general. According to Thurston, in the late Coptic (Ethiopic) texts' fantastically embroidered accounts of St. George, Diocletian has become "King Dadianus" and is called "The Dragon" three times. Thurston adds that "The term dragon appears also in some of the intermediate Latin versions". Finally he reaches the same conclusion as myself: "The dragon now so familiarly connected with St. George first assumes a literal and concrete shape in the *Legenda* of James de Voragine. But we see clearly enough where he comes from. He is simply the tyrant Dadianus ... whom George overcomes, and from whom he rescues that fair Christian maiden typified in the Empress Alexandra."

Chapter Twelve: I am indebted in this section to Boutelle's Heraldry, by J.P. Brooke-Little, Richmond Herald of Arms, and to the Rev. H.S. Reville's The Noble Order of the Garter in the Standard of St. George (April, 1966).

Photographs

A

98